180 DAYS

Crystal E. Emerson,
Bachelor of Science In Secondary Education, Master's of Education, Certification In English, Certification In Special Education.

authorHOUSE®

AuthorHouse™
1663 Liberty Drive
Bloomington, IN 47403
www.authorhouse.com
Phone: 1-800-839-8640

First published by AuthorHouse 9/9/2011

ISBN: 978-1-4634-4668-0 (e)
ISBN: 978-1-4634-4669-7 (hc)
ISBN: 978-1-4634-4670-3 (sc)

Library of Congress Control Number: 2011913637

Printed in the United States of America

Any people depicted in stock imagery provided by Thinkstock are models, and such images are being used for illustrative purposes only. Certain stock imagery © Thinkstock.

This book is printed on acid-free paper.

In Loving Memory of "Dad"
Harold David Hall
October 13, 1922–July 29, 2006

For: W. C., who had faith in my work, respected me, supported me, worked with me, enjoyed a positive and professional rapport with me, and considered my hard work and dedication to the profession an asset to the elementary school in which he was principal.

For: D. D., who supported me emotionally and professionally.

Who Should Read This Book?

President Barack Obama, Hillary Clinton, Laura Bush, Dr. Wayne W. Dyer, Dr. Phil McGraw, Robin McGraw, Oprah Winfrey, John Audi, all PSEA (Pennsylvania State Education Association) attorneys, all attorneys who represent clients in any harassment in the workplace and wrongful discharge cases, all PSEA union representatives, all PSEA union members, all public school teachers, and certainly all public school administrators. I feel Dr. Wayne W. Dyer would say that I am reaching for the sky when I request that the most prestigious people on this planet read my book! The need for people who maintain high ideals and simultaneously remain in powerful positions can help initiate a change. People who believe that integrity and honesty must be implemented at all levels and simultaneously have the financial means to pursue such issues legally can help to make a positive change in our educational system and simultaneously our society.

The law assumes that public school administrators will behave in an ethical manner. The PSEA (Pennsylvania State Education Association) members assume that union representatives will support them during times of professional adversity. This book is a personal account, of a professional position, in which these two assumptions have failed to occur.

Introduction

During the 2002–2003 academic year, Breslin University accepted me into an accelerated education certification program. The local intermediate unit is affiliated with Breslin University, and the program was therefore accelerated because anyone who has an existing Pennsylvania Teaching Certificate (even one not used since 1978) can, after two or three graduate courses, obtain a second teaching certificate—provided one has passed his or her PRAXIS exams.

I actually began graduate school in August 2002, during my daughter Elizabeth's freshmen year of college and my son David's freshmen year of high school. My major was MA in Counseling Psychology, and my very first course was Human Development with Dr. Anna Smith. Dr. Smith enlightened me with her intelligence and her spiritual depth and I was happy that our paths of life had crossed. Our major assignment was to write a self-case analysis and an autobiography. She referred to me as a winner and a "very strong" person capable of becoming self-fulfilled.

I loved the MA major of Psychology, so it was a difficult choice to change majors. However, it was a lengthy and expensive job ticket. I discovered the accelerated program, in which I could earn a Special Education Certification in only two or three courses. There was no student teaching requirement—not even a practicum! I could take all the courses within the following spring and summer sessions and apply for a Special Education teaching position in the fall of 2003. I went for it!

I completed these courses with a friend, Gay Pick, who was employed as an administrator for a local school district. She had worked in public schools all her life and was the most knowledgeable person I had ever met.

Gay Pick was horrified at what was being omitted from these courses. The courses did not take place on campus at Breslin University; they were held at a local building affiliated with the local Intermediate Unit. Later I learned that the professor who had previously taught these courses had suddenly canceled—and the professors who were in charge of instruction were not prepared to cover pertinent information, including IEP writing and progress monitoring. As I was completing my final course in early August of 2003, I was simultaneously going for job interviews for teaching positions.

On July17, 2003, a Thursday afternoon, Gay Pick knocked on my door. I was in the middle of a research paper for my last graduate course for this certification program. This last course was completed on campus at Breslin University. It was informative and lots of work, however I felt I was really learning a great deal about Special Education. Gay informed me that there was an opening at The Souless Area School District, specifically an elementary school called B. C. Patanjali. It was already after lunch, and I was dressed in my shorts wearing almost no facial makeup. I quickly gathered together my credentials and hopped into my car. I realized I could not walk into a school wearing shorts and a skimpy summer top, so I ran back inside, upstairs, and changed into a casual summer dress. Still wearing almost no facial make-up, I drove twenty-five minutes to B. C. Patanjali Elementary School. On the way I passed large farms and stopped at an old-fashioned corner store to ask directions. Finally, I arrived!

I had expected to find a secretary—someone I could simply hand my credential packet over to and wait to hear from a principal about scheduling an interview. Once located, I realized that the school was locked and the parking lot was empty except for one vehicle, a small white car. This was the car of Bill Bellkoe, the principal of B. C. Patanjali Elementary School. Although I did not know this at that moment, Bill would become a highly regarded person in my life, someone I would think of with respect just as I think of Dr. Smith. On that day, Bill was alone in the building which was empty and warm and Bill spotted my car and unlocked the door. I handed him my credentials. He was alone in the building, online using the national teacher application website, REAP, looking for applicants to interview for the newly opened Special Education position in his building. The Regional Education Applicant Placement Program, REAP, is a national educational recruiting service available to anyone seeking employment in a public school district in the state of Pennsylvania.

He said to me, "Come in and sit down; we will talk and consider this our first interview." We talked for approximately fifteen minutes, and he told me to return for a second and more formal interview on Thursday, July 24, 2003. This interview consisted of three principals, two males and one female, and Dr. Lurk, the Supervisor of Special Education. I came home and wrote a thank-you note to Bill Bellkoe, knowing that the interviews had gone well. The note read as follows:

Dear Bill,

I was interviewed today and consider the interview a positive experience. I will be on vacation from Monday, 7/28/03 to Friday, 8/1/03.

Today, as I was driving away from B. C. Patanjali Elementary School, I thought of 100 things I should have said during the interview to sell myself. Hindsight is the key word here.

The students I would be working with at your school are much higher functioning than students who have been diagnosed as having autism or mental retardation. This position is exactly what I am looking for. I want something more academic than the local Intermediate Unit classroom positions offer.

When you asked me to tell me about myself, I should have told you that I am accountable, reliable, responsible, and dedicated. I recently handed in an assignment to Dr. Kola at Breslin University. When she returned it to me, she had written the following comment: "Katrina, Your answers were outstanding—the most complete and salient of all I have received … Thanks for the quality!"

One comforting fact, which you mentioned during the interview, was a comment you made about the Supervisor of Special Education. The fact that she works closely with the special education teachers in preparation of goals and objectives was important to me. I needed to know that it is okay to ask if I am not certain about something.

Thank you for being easy to talk with. By the end of the interview, I felt comfortable and as relaxed as an interviewee can be. You and the others were great to talk with!

Fondly,
Katrina Hall

On Tuesday, August 5, 2003, at 12:30, I had my third and final interview and signed the one-year contract with The Souless Area School District. This interview consisted of Bill Bellkoe, Principal; Dr. Lurk, Supervisor of Special Education; and Dr. James Ryan, Superintendent. Yes! I signed the one year contract with the Souless Area School District!

180 DAYS

August 2003

I was in the middle of writing a paper for one of my graduate courses when Gay Pick knocked on my door informing me of an opening in Special Education at B. C. Patanjali Elementary School, in the Souless Area School District. Gay held the position of Assistant Principal at an elementary school in the a local school district, and had been informed of the opening the second it was posted. I met Gay while taking a course required to complete my Pennsylvania Special Education Certification. Gay was intelligent, kind, and our friendship had grown during our graduate course work. Because Gay was kind enough to inform me of the position, I decided that it was a sign and that I should immediately drive to B. C. Patanjali. I ran upstairs, changed my clothes, brushed my hair, and hopped into the car with a copy of my current resume and credential file.

I was wearing almost no facial makeup, but I expected to simply hand my credential file documents to a secretary. I remember driving up to this beautiful school for the first time and noticing the beautiful farmland that surrounded the school building. I saw only one car in the lot, which belonged not to a secretary, but to Bill Bellkoe, Principal of B. C. Patanjali Elementary School.

Ironically, Bill took my presence as a sign too! As I walked into the building, I noticed many boxes of supplies, new materials awaiting the upcoming school year. Bill informed me that he had just been searching through REAP (The National Applicant Placement Program) applications, and he jokingly informed me that he had not reached "H" names. He also jovially informed me that he sometimes began his work on this website with the letter "Z" because it was not fair to all the people who had last names beginning with letters at the end of the alphabet such as X or Y or Z.

Bill asked me a few questions, looked over my documents, and scheduled an interview!

The scheduled panel interview (the third and final interview) was stressful, with four professionals taking turns firing questions at me! Then, they asked me to wait in a separate room, a small conference room, while they discussed my answers to these questions. After approximately twenty minutes, Bill Bellkoe came into the room and informed me of the good news: the panel felt that I was the best candidate for the position. However, Bill informed me that he would never hire a new teacher without having that teacher meet with the superintendent, Dr. James Ryan, whom for some reason was very late. Bill informed me that Dr. James Ryan was usually very punctual and organized with details. Once again, I was asked to wait for James Ryan to arrive.

Finally, after approximately an hour, James Ryan arrived, shook my hand, and asked me a few questions. James Ryan first asked me how my former coworkers would describe me. I honestly informed him that they would tell him I was dedicated to the profession, and an extremely hard worker to the point of earning the label of anal—obsessive compulsive behavior. He smiled at me and asked me why I wanted to become a teacher. I told him that I had always wanted to be a teacher; truthfully, it was the only career in which I had ever visualized myself. I noticed that he was forlorn and wondered if he had gotten some sort of bad news—which was the reason for his delay and his absence during my interview. Instinctively, I wondered if he had gotten bad news regarding his health. He simply looked sad, but looking through the sadness I observed a kind and sexy man.

I was hired! Just like everything in my life, I was not ready for it—I just dove right in! How could I actually be ready when my crash course in special education did not require a student-teaching segment or a practicum?

Bill gave me the key to my classroom, room 112! I decorated it with posters that Elizabeth, my daughter, helped me draw. My favorite was a quotation from Samuel Longhorn Clemens: "A man who does not read is no better than a man who cannot read." Elizabeth drew these words on a large poster board, and I pointed to it when I explained to the children the value of reading. The other teachers in the building complimented the appearance of my room, considering the fact that I had been hired so late.

Bill and I got along well. I knew what he expected and I did it. There were many challenges, especially in the beginning. My first day of employment was August 18, 2003. This was an induction day for new teachers. Dr. James Ryan, Superintendent, spoke and handed out a poem entitled "Make A Difference." Oh dear! What a sexy man—and single too! I admired him because he seemed very kind, and he certainly was a relaxed public speaker! I immediately laminated this poem and hung it in my classroom 112 at B. C. Patanjali Elementary School. I enjoyed reading the poem because the message made me feel positive!

We Can Make A Difference
If We Choose

One day a man was walking along the beach
when he noticed a figure in the distance.
As he got closer, he realized the figure was that
of a boy picking something up and throwing
it back into the ocean. Approaching the boy, he asked,
"What are you doing?"

The youth replied, "Throwing a starfish into the ocean.
The sun is up and the tide is going out.
If I don't throw them back, they'll die!"

"Son," the man said, "Don't you realize there are
miles and miles of beach and hundreds of starfish?
You can't possibly make a difference!"

After listening politely, the boy bent down, picked up
another starfish and threw it into the surf.
Then, smiling at the man, said,
"I made a difference for that one!"

I thought I was lucky to have been hired into such an excellent school district. Each day I learned more from people who had worked in a public school for twenty or even thirty years. I worked endless hours. We were in the first week of school when Dr. Lurk, Supervisor of Special Education, told me that I would have additional responsibilities within the Souless Area School District. My original assignment was to teach an adaptive health class at Mith Middle School. Also, I would have one homebound student. In addition, my Special Education caseload at B. C. Patanjali was growing faster than imaginable.

The amazing thing about Bill Bellkoe was his ability to teach new teachers how to be productive. I learned more in talking with Bill for fifteen minutes than I had in five college courses. The mornings at B. C. Patanjali Elementary School began with a song over the PA system. The lyrics will be forever etched upon my mind: "Open the door and come on in; I'm so glad to be your friend; you're like a rainbow coming around the bend." As the days passed, that is truly how I felt about Bill. He was there to help me become a better teacher and learn from his thirty-five years of experience, to become my friend, and to be a person whom I could certainly trust.

September 2003

Many challenges came my way during this school year. I was not a reading specialist, and I had never been trained to administer reading assessment tests and place children in books according to diagnostically appropriate reading levels. I was not prepared to write Individual Education Programs (IEPs) and Reevaluation Reports (RRs). Additionally, room 112 contained almost no books or materials. The number of special education students requiring services based on their IEP doubled from four to eight. I was overwhelmed and began working very long hours. However, Bill was feeling frustrated with me and felt that I was not producing. He never said anything to me, but I sensed his negativity toward me. When our paths would coincidentally pass in the hall, or at the copier or in the faculty lunch room, I could feel his frustration and negativity toward me. Instead, he spoke to Dr. Lurk, who sent Diane Ridgedan to assist me in organizing and ordering materials and curriculum. Diane was great! I sensed her positive energy and knew that like me, she worked very hard. We worked well together, and I admired her because she was intelligent, seasoned, and a person of integrity. Furthermore, she had a positive rapport with Bill because they had known one another for many years.

Early in September, Dr. Lurk telephoned me and asked me if I would be willing to teach an adaptive physical education class at Mith Middle School. According to No Child Left Behind (NCLB), this was not legal; I did not have a teaching certificate in physical education! She also asked me if I would use the time before school as my planning period. I innocently informed Dr. Lurk that I was willing to accommodate her requests at Mith and relinquish my planning period. The teaching day at Mith Middle School began one hour earlier than the teaching day at B.C. Patanjali Elementary School. This time difference allowed Dr. Lurk to request that

I teach a Physical Education class in another building, while my coworkers had unassigned time in their schedule. When the more seasoned teachers at B. C. Patanjali Elementary School heard the news, they told me not to do this because everyone had that time. I learned early on that the Soulless Area School District had a very weak union, to say the least!

A few days passed, and I had not heard from Dr. Lurk, so I continued happily working hard at B. C. Patanjali Elementary School. Both Diane and Bill were extremely helpful, and I was learning so much. I loved B. C. Patanjali Elementary School and the teachers and students in that building. Unfortunately, the bad news came: Dr. Lurk told me that I would be spending my afternoon at another school, Mountclair Elementary, teaching small groups of reading and math students. I reminded Dr. Lurk that she had previously asked me to teach an APE (Adaptive Physical Education) class at Mith Middle School. She replied, "Oh! I forgot all about that!" When I observed Dr. Lurk and Diane Ridgedan working together, I knew that Diane was the brains of the operation. Dr. Lurk was a kind person, but I felt that she did not have the aptitude for such an intense professional position. I felt Diane Ridgedan should have held the position of Special Education Supervisor because she was intelligent, strong, and had integrity.

Diane Ridgedan came to B. C. Patanjali one day so that I could follow her to Mountclair Elementary. My instincts told me that this would be the worst part of my day—and it certainly was! The back roads from B. C. Patanjali to Mountclair were surrounded by beautiful woods, and the trees were beginning to change color, which was nice. Occasionally, though, a deer would cross the road, or herds of cows were visible. The scenery consisted of beautiful countryside and farmland. The neighborhoods consisted of many farms and low-income white families.

Diane Ridgedan lead the way, and I followed her through theses windy back roads. We walked inside the school together and down several long corridors until we came to a room—the room! Intuitively, entering this building and this specific classroom felt sad and negative to me. I was introduced to Bertha Both and Shannon Mackley. Bertha Both was a special education teacher, and Shannon Mackley was a Union Representative for the Mountclair Elementary building, and a regular education elementary teacher. Bertha handed Diane my schedule. Diane looked over things and informed Bertha that this was an unfair amount of work: a large number of students and no breaks—not even a bathroom break! Diane instructed Bertha to rewrite the schedule so that I would teach only two reading groups as opposed to three. Bertha informed Diane that she did not feel like retyping the schedule because it was time consuming, and this was already her second time typing it.

Shannon, the Union Representative, looked over the schedule and whispered to me, "You could grieve this." There were no administrators present, just a group of teachers. Therefore my heavy teaching schedule was given to me by another teacher, not an administrator—and certainly not the directive of the special education supervisor! Diane repeated herself and informed Bertha that I should not be responsible for three reading groups—two groups would be plenty. I noticed the distress in Diane's voice and eyes. She certainly had a concern for my heavy workload. She was attempting to explain to Bertha that I also had many responsibilities at B. C. Patanjali. In addition, Dr. Lurk had informed me that I would have one homebound student, for one hour per day, five days per week. Between my students at B. C. Patanjali and my three reading groups at Mountclair, I would go into Mike Bergwise's home and provide daily instruction. Diane Ridgedan was desperately trying to inform Bertha of this unreasonable workload, but Bertha was lazy and wanted to hear nothing of it. Bertha only cared that she had given herself an easy teaching schedule—at my expense. I later learned that Bertha had taken advantage of her aide during the previous academic year (2002–2003) in much the same way she would take advantage of me during the 2003–2004 academic year.

Diane asked Bertha how she had planned to have simultaneous group instruction in one room. Bertha informed Diane that she had already asked the custodians to set up a divider in the back of the classroom. The divider in this large classroom was symbolic of the lazy behavior of Bertha Both, and it was ludicrous that administrators had no idea how much I was being taken advantage of in this situation. The reality of this divider was that I would be teaching several students at a time inside a very small segment of Bertha's room. Simultaneously, Bertha had one or no students and 75 percent of her room, while I was inundated with eleven very struggling students, a scripted reading program, no bathroom breaks, no lunch break, and a devious administrator who hated me from the start! Diane could not believe that Bertha was going to stick me behind this divider and told Bertha not to give me so many of her caseload students—but Bertha was lazy and did not listen to Diane. Diane unfortunately could not persuade Bertha to be more fair and not to take advantage of me. This entire detailed scheduled had been planned out by one lazy teacher with no input from Brenda Craiger, the Principal of Mountclair Elementary School, and certainly no input from Dr. Lurk, the Supervisor of Special Education.

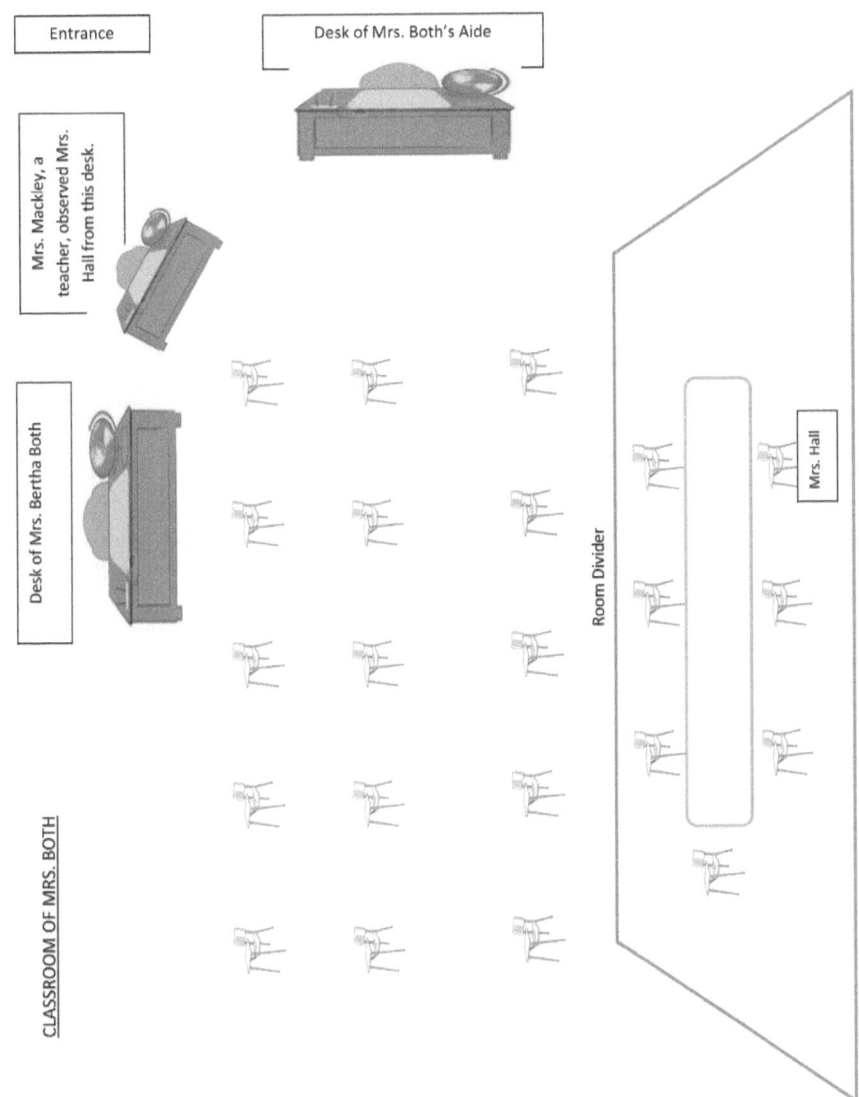

Illustration of Bertha Both's Classroom with a divider.

Unfair Schedules

Here is a breakdown of Mrs. Bertha Both's schedule. Bertha had a tremendous amount of unassigned time during her school day.

Monday Schedule for Bertha Both

9:00–9:30—Unassigned. Bertha Both found it necessary to have coffee and relax before her relaxing schedule every Monday. She began her day with thirty minutes of free and unassigned time!

9:30–10:10—Math 5: 9 students—Bertha made her groups of learning-disabled students large so that she could give herself free time. She could have taught a group of four and a group of five. Instead, she put all nine students together to free up her time! It is obvious that she looked at scheduling more than ability when instructing her learning disabled students.

10:10–10:55—Reading Group A: 2 students—Bertha only had two students in her room at a time. Due to the fact that I was assigned to B. C. Patanjali for such a short period of time, it was necessary for me to simultaneously have some students working on math while others were completing a reading lesson. How nice of Bertha to only assign two students at a time to her part of the room.

10:55–11:15—Math 1: 1 student—Bertha gave herself a slot of time with only one student because she was well aware that this student had severe health problems. If Bertha assigned this child to her schedule (alone—not with any other students in that math group), she knew that she was frequently providing herself with another planning period because this student was frequently absent, therefore, Bertha Both frequently had another free time slot in her schedule!

11:15–11:45—Math 2: 2 students—Only two children in Bertha's room at this time.

11:45–12:15—Lunch—More unassigned time in Bertha's schedule! She needed lunch! I felt she needed to educate herself on maintaining a healthy life style which included exercise and eating the proper amounts of low-fat foods.

12:15–1:00—Math 3: 2 students—Only two children in her room for forty-five minutes! How easy is that?

1:00–1:45—Math 4: Inclusion for only two students.

During this period of time, Bertha went into Shannon Mackley's classroom. Shannon did all the work while Bertha just stood there. Shannon prepared all the lesson plans, instructed, and graded all the papers. Bertha just stood there—she did not do any work for forty-five minutes. Surprise, surprise!

The only day that Bertha brought these two children and another child back to classroom at Mountclair was the day when Brenda Craiger tipped her off about the walk-through observation of Dr. Marcel Nulldick! On that day Bertha located a third child, brought them into her room, and taught them a math lesson—but only because Brenda Craiger had secretly instructed her to do so. After all, how would it look if Bertha was standing in Shannon's classroom doing nothing while Katrina was stuffed behind a divider with eleven students? I wonder how Bertha got the third student. I am certain that Brenda Craiger informed Bertha that two students would be an insufficient number due to the fact that Dr. Marcel Nulldick would notice the imbalance of schedules. I knew the instant Brenda Craiger and Dr. Marcel Nulldick walked through the door that this entire walk-through observation had been prearranged by Brenda Craiger and staged by Bertha Both!

As Brenda Craiger stood there, I could feel the hatred that she had for me! The negativity was strong, and her aura was yellow and brown due to her negative emotional condition. Dr. Marcel Nulldick just stood there beside her, continuing to smile, although he looked a little nervous. I felt sympathy for them because they lacked emotional intelligence!

1:50–2:30—Reading Group E: 4 students.

2:30–3:00—Reading Mastery with Katrina—This was the clincher! I had no idea Bertha could get away with unassigned time based on a big lie!

READING MASTERY WITH KATRINA!!!!!!!!!!!!!!!!

The first time I saw this statement, I was outraged and astounded! It was the day I quickly walked to the copier, made the copy, and returned the schedule to the bulletin board; no one saw me do so! Another thirty minutes of unassigned time in Bertha's schedule! I cringed the day I first discovered this because Bertha Both *never* helped me! If she had time to help me with one of those reading groups then it should have been her reading group to instruct—not mine! Diane Ridgedan tried to tell Bertha Both this, but to no avail because Bertha was lazy! Brenda Craiger knew Bertha had this unassigned time in her schedule, and she underhandedly and secretively allowed this because she ran a school of favorites.

3:00–3:30—Plan time, progress monitoring, consult with aide. Another thirty minutes of unassigned time.

Mondays for Bertha Both were actually fairly relaxing. When her 11:15–10:55 student was absent, she had almost three hours per day of unassigned time! She did nothing during inclusion, and she nothing during her unassigned time. With all this free unassigned time during the school day, Bertha took nothing home and never had to stay late—she was out the door the second the buses left the parking lot!

Tuesday Schedule for Bertha Both
9:15–9:30—Unassigned

9:30–10:00—Math 1: 1 student—The student was frequently absent due to severe issues.

10:00–10:45—Reading Group A: 2 students.

10:50–11:30—Math 5: 9 students.

11:30–12:00—LUNCH—Unassigned.

12:00–12:45—Math 3: 2 students.

12:45–1:20—Unassigned—Plan time; consult with aid.

1:20–1:45—Inclusion Math 4: 2 students—Inclusion in Shannon Mackley's room.

1:45–2:30—Reading Group E: 4 students.

2:30–3:10—Math 2: 2 students.

3:10–3:35—Unassigned. Reading Mastery with Katrina! Amazing—Bertha gave herself twenty-five minutes of essentially unassigned time! She was so very kind to herself!

Tuesdays for Bertha Both were very relaxing and slow paced! She had two hours and fifteen minutes of unassigned time when her math student was absent, plus forty-five minutes of inclusion, for a total of three hours of relaxation in her day every Tuesday!

Wednesday Schedule for Bertha Both
9:15–9:50—Math 2: 2 students.

9:50–10:30—Math 5: 9 students.

10:30–11:00—Math 4 Inclusion: 2 students.

11:00–11:30—Lunch

11:30–12:15—Reading Group E: 4 students.

12:15–1:00—Reading Group A: 2 students.

1:00–1:40—Math 3: 2 students.

1:45–2:15—Math 1: 1 student—Student was frequently absent due to severe illness.

2:20–2:50—Reading Mastery with Katrina—essentially unassigned time.

2:50–3:30—Unassigned: Plan Time; Progress Monitoring; Consult with Aide.

Wednesdays for Bertha Both were especially relaxing in the afternoon. After 1:40 she was free! Total unassigned time, plus inclusion, is three hours and twenty-five minutes! This was an outrage!

Thursday Schedule for Bertha Both
9:15–10:00—Reading Group E: 4 students.

10:00–10:45—Reading Group A: 2 students.

10:45–11:15—Lunch.

11:20–12:00—Math 5: 9 students.

12:05–12:45—Math 3: 2 students.

12:45–1:05—Unassigned—Plan Time.

1:05–1:45—Math 4 Inclusion: 2 students—In Shannon Mackley's classroom.

1:50–2:30—Math 2: 2 students.

2:30–2:45—Unassigned.

2:45–3:15—Math 1: 1 student—Student was frequently absent.

3:15–3:35—Reading Mastery with Katrina!— Essentially unassigned time.

Ludicrous! On Thursday after 2:30, Bertha gave herself a nice break until 4:00PM!

Friday Schedule for Bertha Both

9:15–9:50—Reading Group E: 4 students.

9:50–10:20—Math 2: 2 students.

10:20–10:50—Math 5: 9 students.

10:50–11:30—Math 4 Inclusion: 2 students—In Shannon Mackley's classroom.

11:45–12:25—Math 3: 2 students.

12:25–12:55—Reading Group A: 2 students.

1:00–1:30—Lunch.

1:30–2:10—Unassigned; Plan Time.

2:10–2:30—Math 1: 1 student—The student was frequently absent.

2:30–2:45—Unassigned; Consult with Aide; Progress Monitoring.

2:45–3:35—Reading Mastery with Katrina— Essentially unassigned time.

Amazing! I think from this schedule we can surmise that Bertha Both was really exhausted by Friday afternoon. It was necessary for her to provide herself with a solid three-hour consecutively scheduled block of unassigned time! Brenda Craiger must not have noticed that Bertha Both gave herself a three-hour break at my expense! She gave herself a three hour break in addition to her lunch and inclusion—which were also free time in Bertha's schedule! Bertha would frequently miss going into Shannon's classroom for inclusion, but that was okay with Brenda Craiger because Bertha Both was a favorite! After I took a copy of Bertha's schedule to Dr. Marcel Nulldick in December, they were reprimanded. I hope this schedule resulted in professional ramifications and I hope they received a negative memo in their file—a strike against them.

Katrina Hall's Schedule—This schedule was prepared by Dr. Lurk on 10/21/2003. I was given no lunch and no planning. Therefore, my schedule was in violation of my contract.

Monday through Friday:
9:00–11:30—Instruct students at B. C. Patanjali.

12:00–12:15—Travel time.

12:15–12:55—Homebound instruction.

12:55–1:10—Travel time.

1:10–1:20—Set up for instruction at Mountclair Elementary School.

1:20–2:20—Reading group or math group.

2:05–2:45—Reading group or math group.

2:45–3:30—Reading group or math group.

3:30–4:00—Consult with teachers at Mountclair Elementary School.

My head was swimming by the time I left B. C. Patanjali Elementary School!

Prior to Christmas break, I informed Dr. Marcel Nulldick that I had no planning time and no lunch time built into my schedule. He did not remove any of my responsibilities! He simply typed the schedule below. This was inane because I had B. C. Patanjali students in my classroom from the time they got off of their school bus until I left the building. It was not possible to instruct six to eight children in math and reading in the small amount of time allotted in this ridiculous schedule! I don't care how Dr. Marcel retyped things—I know I had at least thirty minutes less than my contracted unassigned time, because Bill Bellkoe told me so. Also, I know

I had insufficient travel time because a union representative told me so. Dr. Marcel Nulldick could have retyped my schedule an endless number of times, but until someone removed some of these responsibilities, nothing changed. I would like to have seen anyone walk in my shoes, day after day, and deal with such a ridiculous workload. When I compared my schedule to that of Bertha Both's, I became filled with anger and resentment. She had no right to take advantage of me—and have her principal Brenda Craiger condone her actions! Why was Bertha Both allowed to take advantage of me? I have frequently heard that God would not give you more than you could handle. This was it—I had reached my limit!

Katrina Hall's Schedule -— This schedule was prepared by Dr. Marcel Nulldick on 1/13/04.

Monday through Friday:
8:20–8:50—Meet with teachers at B. C. Patanjali.

8:55–9:15—Planning time.

9:15–11:10—Instructional time for B. C. Patanjali.

11:10–11:40—Planning time.

11:40–12:10—Lunch.

12:10–12:25—Travel time.

12:25–1:05—Homebound instruction with Mike W.

1:05–1:20—Travel time.

1:20–3:35—Reading Group Instruction: 11 students.

3:35–4:00—Meet with Mountclair teachers.

Here is a detailed breakdown of my Monday through Friday.

8:20–8:50—Meet with teachers at B. C. Patanjali. *Dr. Marcel Nulldick is not allowed to assign anything to me during this time period because everyone has this time to themselves and it violates my teaching contract.*

8:55–9:15—Planning time. *I could not use this time for my planning time because I brought children into my classroom for instruction immediately after they got off of their school bus. It was the only way I could provide the required amount of time according to the IEP and state regulations.*

9:15–11:10—Instructional time for students at B. C. Patanjali. *This was not enough time! It was not possible because my B. C. Patanjali caseload increased as the academic year progressed. It was very difficult to instruct math and reading groups simultaneously. Why did I have to teach reading and math simultaneously? Compare my schedule to that of Bertha Both!*

11:10–11:40—Planning time. *I could not use this time for planning because I had students in my room.*

11:40–12:10—Lunch. *Many days I allowed the students to eat with me in my room while we simultaneously worked on assignments.*

12:10–12:25—Travel time. *It was very tough to actually be in my car and have materials for my afternoon packed and organized by 12:10.*

12:25–1:05—Homebound instruction with Mike W.

1:05–1:20—Travel time. *It was always necessary to drive fast!*

1:20–3:35—Reading group instruction: 11 students. *No breaks! Straight instruction with scripted reading materials!*

3:35–4:00—Meet with Mountclair teachers. *Dr. Marcel Nulldick violated my contract when he wrote this into my schedule because everyone has this time to themselves.*

How he dared rewrite my schedule so that it appeared to have a planning and a lunch! How dare he do so! It made me so very angry—he simply retyped my schedule! He should have redistributed my professional responsibilities. Compare my schedule to that of Bertha Both! Compare Bertha Both's unassigned time to my overloaded schedule. The schedule comparison was an outrage! Furthermore, the fact that Bertha Both's home base school was located near the residence of my homebound student had been noticed by several other teachers. She had free time and she was close by—let the lazy person with free time have a homebound student in the middle of her school day! Dr. Marcel Nulldick could not understand my level of frustration. The schedule comparison alone was enough to make anyone fill with anger and rage. I was taken advantage of to the extreme, and it was all condoned by a principal! I was the victim of sabotage and undermining for 180 days!

Scripted reading books were handed to me for three different levels! Bertha Both instructed me to take them home and read the teacher manuals. I informed Bertha that this was not possible because I was taking home hours of preparation work from B. C. Patanjali Elementary School—and I would certainly not have time to do both. Furthermore, I had been handed numerous folders of documents written about my homebound student. Dr. Lurk had directed me to thoroughly review these documents over the weekend. She informed me that his updated IEP (Individualized Education Program) was not in that specific folder, but it would be given to me in the near future. I was not familiar with scripted reading, but at first glance it appeared to be a program that would make any student hate to read! I was truly a bibliophile, and my heart sank when I originally viewed the scripted reading materials. There are so many exciting ways to develop lifelong readers—students who desire to read for pleasure—but this scripted reading program was certainly NOT one of them!

All this had occurred, and I still had not met Brenda Craiger. I was specifically told that I would meet her on September 9, 2003, Tuesday, after I had completed my morning responsibilities at B. C. Patanjali and my homebound student assignment. Also, this was the scheduled Back-To-School night for B. C. Patanjali Elementary School! —busy day! Therefore I worked with my learning-disabled students at B. C. Patanjali Elementary School, which I loved. If only I could have stayed at B. C. Patanjali all day and instruct those children—how perfect this would have been! Then on I went to my homebound student. On this specific day I was supposed to meet the speech therapist at Mike's home, however, she did not arrive at Mike's home during the designated time frame. I certainly could not stay longer than scheduled because I was scheduled to talk with Brenda Craiger before I instructed my three scripted reading groups. I left Mike's home at my scheduled time and drove to Mountclair Elementary School. This was only my second time to drive to the school, and I was not familiar with these windy back roads. I was not certain how far down the road I would drive before I would see the school. However, I did not want to be late because I had heard that Brenda Craiger was a stickler for being on time, and if I had not arrived on time she could formally reprimand me.

I hastily drove down this road, not even aware that there was a motorcycle behind me! Suddenly I saw the sign for Mountclair Elementary School, and I slammed on my breaks. The man on the motorcycle flew over my car and landed on the road in a pool of his own blood. I had no cell phone, and therefore I could not telephone 911. A van driving the opposite direction stopped—coincidentally, it was Mike's speech therapist, and she happened to have a cell phone. She called 911, and a police officer and ambulance arrived on the scene in a few moments. I was hysterical because I thought I had killed another human being. The police officer made small talk in an attempt to calm me. The ambulance driver told me he felt more sorry for me than the man whom they were loading into the ambulance. The paramedics assured me that the motorcycle driver would be just fine! The police officer was kind and physically flawless, ultimately an Adonis! I also thought he was looking at me as though he were attracted to me. Then I saw an overweight female walking out of the school. She was wearing a low-cut navy blue dress so that one could see her cleavage! I thought how inappropriate this low-cut dress was, considering she was an administrator in a public elementary school. Her hair was jet black—obviously dyed. She walked up to me and introduced herself as Brenda Craiger, the Principal of Mountclair Elementary School. She attempted to comfort me, but I was beyond comforting. She walked me into the building and told me to rest in the nurse's office. The nurse was kind and gave me a bottle of water. She also asked me if there was anyone she could call. I told her there was no one and that I would be fine. From that day on the school nurse and I developed a professional and personal rapport. Brenda Craiger instructed me to go home for the remainder of the school day. This was the single act of kindness that Brenda Craiger bestowed upon me during the entire 2003–2004 academic year. I informed Brenda that I could not go home because it was the scheduled Back-To-School night at B. C. Patanjali Elementary School. She replied, "Oh well; people have missed it due to less of an excuse than this!"

September flew by because I was working endless hours in an attempt to handle this unfair and overwhelming workload. It would have been difficult for an experienced teacher to deal with this, but I had no experience! One day in mid-September, Diane Ridgedan was helping me organize reading materials for my students at B. C. Patanjali Elementary School. Diane expressed, "It is taking every bit of my thirty years of experience to help you get this program organized."

On September 30, 2003, Dr. James Ryan, the Superintendent, walked into classroom 112 at B. C. Patanjali Elementary School, followed by Bill Bellkoe. I was shocked and nervous! When he walked through my classroom door, I looked up from my reading book. We made eye contact, and he smiled and said, "Hi!" I was so nervous I did not return his smile or his greeting. Later, when I thought about this, I felt sad that I had not greeted him in a more friendly and positive manner, because I certainly received positive vibrations from him. However, the panic that rose inside of me when these two gentlemen walked through the door prevented me from any positive social interaction. Some of my students were in the middle of individual assignments, and simultaneously I was completing a reading lesson with my very low students. Everyone was working hard, engaged, and in control! Dr. James Ryan liked what he observed and left behind a picture and a note on my desk. The illustration included a picture of the old-fashioned, one-room school house, a teacher, and students running in the door of the school. The caption read, "A school is four walls with tomorrow inside." The note read, "Katrina, Enjoyed my visit to your class! Nice job! Have a great year! JR." I imagine it is rather ironic that the superintendent himself told me I was doing a "nice job"!

"A school is four walls with tomorrow inside."

Schoolhouse illustration from the Superintendent.

This was the day (September 30th of 2003–during the walk through observation) that I won over Bill Bellkoe. From this day on, he, Bill Bellkoe, the principal of B. C. Patanjali, thought highly of me. Diane informed me that Bill was not an easy principal to win over—if Bill thought highly of me, I deserved it!

August and September were filled with new experiences, frustrations, long hours of hard work, intense professional responsibilities and sleepless nights. I needed to learn everything! I needed to learn how to prepare special education documents, use a computer, write sufficient lesson plans, present scripted reading lessons, and more. The list was infinite and overwhelming. I was taken advantage of by Bertha Both and simultaneously undermined and sabotaged by Brenda Craiger.

I loved my job at B. C. Patanjali and hated my job at Mountclair. Each day I would leave Mountclair as quickly as possible and drive back to B. C. Patanjali Elementary. Of course I wanted to leave the building where I was surrounded with unpleasant and stressful situations. Of course I wanted to return to the building where the other teachers and the principal had a positive rapport with me.

One day in September, Bertha told me that I was supposed to stay at Mountclair until 4:00 PM. I explained to Bertha that Bill Bellkoe had informed me that I could return to B. C. Patanjali as soon as I was finished instructing my reading groups. I told Bill Bellkoe what Bertha had said, and he replied, "Well, Bertha Both is not your boss; I am." Behind my back, of course, Bertha told Brenda about this conversation, and Brenda called me into her office and told me that I had to stay at Mountclair until 4:00 PM. I hated going into her office, where there were leftover negative vibes and negative energy from formerly hated and tortured teachers. Each time I walked into her office, I tried to prepare myself for the much-expected tirade! Our meetings were always disconcerting to me because she was consistently rude. The sense of wrongfulness was so strong that I swore Brenda Craiger was from the dark side!

I explained to Brenda that I could not get any work done because all of my materials and my computer were in my classroom 112 at B. C. Patanjali Elementary School. I also told her that Bill had given me permission to return to B. C. Patanjali after 3:20 PM. I reminded her that I was not leaving to go home—just to get my work completed! She replied, "Well, I didn't think you were trying to get over on anyone." Brenda was her usual petulant self! I could feel the hate and distaste she had toward me! She was firm and told me I must stay there until 4:00 PM. I explained to her that this meant that I would arrive at B. C. Patanjali Elementary even later and then it would be necessary for me to spend even more of my evening working late. She didn't care—she just wanted to make me do the opposite of the directive that had come from Bill Bellkoe! I told Diane Ridgedan the situation, and she replied, "Brenda only did this because Bill gave you permission to leave at 3:20 PM." The tyrant, Brenda Craiger, won!

One day, soon after Brenda Craiger had directed me to stay at Mountclair until 4:00 PM, Shannon Mackley came back behind the divider at 3:55 PM. She didn't say anything—she just looked at me. I said "Hi."

She replied, "Oh! I didn't know whether you were still here or not!" Shannon didn't say anything after that—she simply walked out of Bertha's classroom. I knew instantly that Brenda Craiger had directed Shannon Mackley (behind my back of course) to check up on me. The ironic part of this was that Shannon Mackley was a Union Representative for the Mountclair Elementary Building! I had heard that the Souless School District had a weak union—Gay Pick had informed me of this. However, this was ludicrous—the principal, —yours truly Brenda Craiger, the tyrant, shared confidential information with a teacher—Shannon Mackley—who was the building's Union Representative. Brenda had no right to tell Shannon that I had been directed to stay at Mountclair until 4:00 PM. It was none of Shannon's business! The internal rage and anger rose inside me, and I wanted to get away from Mountclair as quickly as I could!

October 2003

One day in October, 2003, Brenda Craiger had complained about me to Dr. Lurk. Who knows what this principal said about me? Dr. Lurk informed me that she would not hire an extra teacher in October, "Because you get the leftovers!" Dr. Lurk was giving me a reason why she should not fire me! Well guess what? People who live in glass houses should not throw stones. Dr. Lurk was fired in December 2003! How dare she have one thought of incompetence about me—it was my first year, and I had everything to learn, with basically no mentor. Dr. Lurk had observed me early in October, liked what she saw, but never bothered to complete the formal observation form! Therefore no documentation of the proficient formal observation existed. Dr. Lurk told Diane Ridgedan what a great job I was doing with my instruction. Then, because Brenda Craiger hated me, Dr. Lurk was going to take her side! I feel that Dr. Lurk was incompetent because I asked her a question about an IEP (Individualized Education Program), and she informed me, "If you have any more questions about IEPs, please ask Diane Ridgedan, because I don't know that much about them." Then she made a lame asinine excuse for her incompetence: "In my position I really don't have many occasions to write them." Her title was Supervisor of Special Education! Therefore she was supposed to critique and scrutinize the Individualized Education Programs and Reevaluation Reports (legal documents which special education teachers are required to write) from the special education teachers whom she supervised. She really should not have admitted that to me. It made me think less of her. I was shocked and considered this a professional outrage, as well as a disgrace to the special education department and to the district.

During October I had several friends and acquaintances working in the

Souless Area School District, including the janitors and the teachers at B.C. Patanjali Elementary School. They became my evening conversationalists, my friends, and simultaneously my support system. They informed me that the general consensus in this district was a hatred for African Americans and for Catholics. I thought seriously about these accusations because I had attended two Catholic universities, one as an undergraduate and another for a portion of my graduate work. I wondered if this was the reason why Brenda Craiger hated me so intensely. Could something this inane be a contributing factor? As I looked around, I did not see an African American in this entire school district! Certainly there existed a lack of cultural diversity in this backwoods public school district! Did the administrators actually think that all Catholics and all African Americans had nothing to offer their district? This was sad. As I lamented the lack of cultural diversity, I thought of how many instances African Americans were refused interviews just because their skin was a different color than that of the administrators in the Souless Area School District. It must have been true because every single teacher in the district was Caucasian. And how could they dislike Catholics? I had attended four universities—two were Catholic universities and two were state universities. The Catholic universities had higher admission standards and offered more difficult course work than that of the state universities. What was the deal? Were Catholics too intelligent for them?

On October 23, 2003, Bill Bellkoe formally observed me at B. C. Patanjali Elementary School. This was my first formal observation during the academic year. Only three formal observations were required, but after things became intense, I was formally observed eight times! If things had gone smoothly, I would have been formally observed three times in total by Bill Bellkoe at B. C. Patanjali—none from Brenda Craiger! Perhaps Dr. Marcel Nulldick would have joined Bill Bellkoe during one formal observation, but that would have been that. The observation categories included professionalism, preparation, teaching techniques, and pupil reaction. The codes upon which I was graded were as follows.

4—Competency fully demonstrated

3—Competency demonstrated but could be further developed

2—Competency partially demonstrated

1—Competency not demonstrated

Bill Bellkoe stated that I was either a 4 or a 3 in every category! In addition to these numbers, Bill Bellkoe wrote the following notes on the formal observation form: "These ratings are based on impressions outside of this formal observation. I observed a nice exchange with Gary's mother in the lobby this morning. You spend a lot of time making and gathering materials to meet your students' needs. You do a nice job of encouragement. Make sure that you do not over encourage, but use reinforcement for genuine improvement." (This was what I loved about Bill Bellkoe: he always started with something positive—an accomplishment to be proud of—and then he suggested a change for the better. He truly knew how to make new teachers become more proficient teachers! It was so easy because I always knew what he wanted, and I just did it!) On the second page of this formal observation, under the category entitled "Areas of Strength," Bill Bellkoe listed the following:

You were telling Gary the why of the activity that you did.

You made the following statement to the student: "The purpose of going over vocabulary first is so that you will know each word when you come to it as you read."

You made the following statement: "You answered all the questions correctly, which means that you are not only reading the words but you are understanding what you have read."

You read the page as a model reading slowly with expression. You used the highlighter and pointed with your pencil.

Nice smooth transition between students. Agenda for Tim on the board helped him know what to do and feel comfortable.

You are working on all the problems that Gary had (i.e., I noticed that you are making some numbers backward … Sit up; you can't read with your head down).

In another important section, entitled "Teacher/Supervisor Comments," Bill Bellkoe wrote the following statement: "I was pleased with the learning that was taking place in your room. The students were productively engaged even though Gary is a high-maintenance student who is very needy in terms of individual attention. Your choice of learning objectives for him were right on target. You also did an excellent job of explaining why he had to do each activity, which seemed to be motivating for Gary." Yes, this was a wonderfully positive first formal observation!

On Wednesday, October 29, 2003, Bill Bellkoe and I had our post-observation conference. Bill reviewed the positive qualities that he saw in me as a teacher. He emphasized the fact that I was able to read aloud slowly to the students and still have expression in my voice. He felt this was very difficult to do and that I had done an excellent job. Bill gave me the sheet to sign; after he and I signed it, the original went to the district office. The observation report closed with one final statement: The summary of the performance of this teacher during the classroom observation could be marked as satisfactory, marginal, or unsatisfactory. Satisfactory was checked, of course! Bill Bellkoe thought I was a strong teacher with many positive qualities.

I was elated when I left his office and could not wait to show Diane Ridgedan my copy of this most significant formal observation! I knew this was an important document to hang on to—but at that time I did not realize how significant this document would become.

I celebrated that day. I reported off sick from my afternoon assignment! My homebound student was ill, and I was informed that I should not come to his home. It was a B. C. Patanjali only day—the way I wished every day could be! No way was I going to ruin this perfect day by going over to the Mountclair abuse behind the divider! I was very happy and I was going to stay that way by not going to Mountclair! I deserved it!

My Christmas Present
December 2003

On December 18, 2003 I gave Bill Bellkoe a Christmas card that contained the following note:

Dear Bill,

Thanks for all your support this year. It has been rough to say the least. Thank you for allowing me to shadow Mary—two classes observing Mary helped me a great deal. I know you are looking out for me—thanks. I am glad I have had the opportunity to work under you; you are a strong leader—that is why B. C. Patanjali is such a fine school. Have a great holiday!

Fondly,
Katrina

When Bill read this note, he told me that he felt that I was saying good-bye to him forever, instead of saying good-bye for Christmas break. Frankly, things were so hatefully intense at Mountclair that I wanted to run away from The Souless School District forever. I continued to love my job and the people and certainly the students at B. C. Patanjali Elementary—in spite of Mountclair.

On December 19, 2003, I had a casual conversation with Bill Bellkoe during which he referred to me as a "good teacher." Considering all the professional and emotional adversity that I endured during the 2003–2004 academic year, hearing those words from this man whom I so highly respected kept me going! Diane Ridgerdan was always there to remind me that Bill Bellkoe was not an easy administrator to win over. If Bill thought you were a good teacher—than you were a good teacher! This was the positive statement that I needed to focus on when dealing with the tyrant Brenda Craiger!

Snow Storm

On, Tuesday, January 27, 2004 there was a terrible snowstorm. I could not believe that the Souless Area School District was not closed that day! I started out, and my car would not go up the hill going away from B. C. Patanjali Elementary School. When I tried driving away from my home, and driving toward Mountclair, my car just would not go in that direction. How symbolic was that? Somehow I managed to drive back to B. C. Patanjali Elementary School. I called Shelly Mitchel, Acting Supervisor of Special Education, on the telephone, but she was not in her office. I then found Bill Bellkoe, who told me about another road that I could take. I was hoping he would tell me not to leave B. C. Patanjali under the circumstances. These windy back roads were drifted shut, and I was in need of new tires! Plus, while driving toward Mountclair Elementary School, I was simultaneously driving farther away from my home! However, I listened to Bill and drove to my homebound student's home; it took one hour. I was sliding and spinning! From my homebound student's home I telephoned B. C. Patanjali and asked Bill to call Mountclair to inform them that I would be late. When I arrived at Mountclair, more than one hour late, I went directly to Brenda Craiger's office. I wondered how she would treat me, knowing that I had driven to her school in a blizzard! It was the second time that she was kind to me. I was flabbergasted! She was actually kind to me! What was that about? Was it phony?

On Monday, February 02, 2003, I had a lengthy, casual conversation with Bill Bellkoe. I told him how much Brenda Craiger hated me and wondered why Bill and Brenda hated one another—their professional animosity was well-known throughout this small school district. I wondered what had happened between the two administrators, many years ago, and why Bill Bellkoe thought so highly of Brenda's spouse but hated Brenda herself. I sincerely felt that I was the victim of a lengthy and ongoing animosity between these two administrators. I truly was a victim caught in the middle of a political battle that had begun long before I had ever applied to the Souless Area School District. Otherwise, they would have agreed on a reading program that was best for all the children in both buildings—and therefore decreased my preparation time. Furthermore, they would have agreed to allow me to return to my home base where my computer and materials were stored to decrease my hours of personal time on the job. If they had worked together, my professional life would have been easier. I lived with a professional dichotomy, attempting to keep everyone happy. Bill Bellkoe and I discussed this, and he was well aware that I had four different people to please: himself, Brenda Craiger, Marcel Nulldick, and Shelly Mitchel—four different professionals with four very different sets of professional expectations for me! I was given an impossible schedule that violated my teaching contract, and I was also asked to keep four very different people happy.

When I spoke to Bill Bellkoe about how intensely Brenda Craiger hated me, I informed him, "She is such a vindictive person; once you are on Brenda's bad side, you may as well forget it."

Bill replied, "Things worked out with other personal situations in your life, and things will work out with Brenda too." I wondered if he sincerely believed that—did Bill actually think Brenda would let up? Did he actually think that I could win her over?

100 Days

On Monday, February 09, 2004, I talked with Kara Keep, my mentor, on the telephone that evening at home. She knew things were intensely negative with Brenda Craiger, and I informed Kara that I didn't think I could finish the academic year and continue to endure the torture being dished out by Brenda Craiger. Kara was so encouraging! She told me I could do it because that day was day number 100! Kara reminded me that we were more than halfway there! Kara sent me a card that said, "Hang in there!"

I frequently felt I could not continue—not one more day of sabotage, undermining, lies, victimization, and the resulting emotional outrage of being wrongfully convicted! Not one more day! I knew I could not resign in the middle of the year because I would not get hired by any other school district! I also knew that I could not get fired, or else I would never get hired. I was a dreamer. Sometimes I would pretend that I was making a movie about a public school teacher, and a renowned film producer hired me to work for one year to help produce a movie about public school systems. I would visualize the film production personnel joking with me regarding the fact that I was not supposed to get fired—I was just supposed to bring practical knowledge to produce a realistic movie. The title of the movie was going to be _180 DAYS_.

My experiences were more than devastating, but adding some humor sometimes helped me. I tried to learn from and observe the behaviors of the administrators and the one teacher who victimized me. I knew we were all connected, and I knew that every thought and action or behavior impacted millions of other people. I knew that when they thought they were hurting me, they were only hurting themselves.

I knew that every thought was a force in the universe. I knew that every behavior (positive or negative) impacted millions of other people. Therefore, I observed the behaviors of all professionals in the Souless Area School District!

The Educator Misconduct Codes

There is in existence a list of Educator Misconduct Complaint Codes. The Codes of Conduct include such areas as immorality, incompetence, intemperance, persistent and willful violation of school laws, cruelty, negligence, crimes and misdemeanors involving moral turpitude, or violations of the code of conduct. During the 2003–2004 academic year, I feel that Brenda Craiger violated every single one of these codes, at my professional expense. To top it off, the Souless School District hired an assistant superintendent, Marcel Nulldick, who came on board officially in November 2003. As the 2003–2004 academic year progressed, I watched Marcell Nulldick lie—just out and out LIE--to cover the actions of Brenda Craiger. I frequently wondered what would have happened if Dr. Marcel Nulldick (the first Assistant Superintendent in the Souless Area School District) had not been hired. I felt Dr. James Ryan, Superintendent, was much too kind to let Brenda Craiger treat any teacher this way. Besides, Dr. James Ryan looked at me the way a man looked at a woman when he found her physically attractive! Diane Ridgedan told me that Dr. Marcel Nulldick had been hired to perform Dr. Ryan's "dirty work"; therefore, if anyone were to be dismissed or reprimanded, Dr. Marcel Nulldick would have the privilege of doing so!

The educator misconduct categories of criminal charges performed by Brenda Craiger include moral turpitude, immorality, cruelty, negligence, and persistent and willful violation of school laws. The criminal behavior of Brenda Craiger, Principal, and the lies of Marcel Nulldick, Assistant Superintendent, intentionally impeded my ability to work in another school district. On December 19, 2003, I contacted Dr. Marcel Nulldick and originally informed him of the incident on September 5, 2003, when

Brenda allowed another teacher to determine my teaching schedule. Brenda was reprimanded by Marcel for this behavior, and she hated me for informing him of her misconduct. Following my meeting with Marcel Nulldick on December 10, 2003, Brenda Craiger became angry with me; whenever I was in the same room with Brenda, I could feel her intense hate and the level of anger that she felt toward me was so thick that it was tangible! The sense of wrongfulness always surrounded her—she carried an aura of negativity with her at all times. Many instances occurred during the 2003–2004 academic year in which Brenda Craiger shared confidential information about me with a certain group of favorite teachers in her building.

When she was alone with me, she was always rude and used sharp and rude tones during her conversations. I cried every time I was alone with her. Brenda Craiger was consistently perverse and petulant, and I could sense her negativity toward me a mile away!

According to PDE (Pennsylvania Department of Education) the Pennsylvania Professional Standards and Practices Commission has identified and defined the term "Cruelty" as an established Code of Cconduct. Any public school employee working as a teacher or an administrator in the state of Pennsylvania who violates these Codes Of Conduct could be professionally disciplined and possibly dismissed for unprofessional behavior. Unfortunately for me, after having spoken with numerous lawyers and attorneys, I have learned that if an administrator violates these Codes of Conduct, they will most likely get away with their behavior. If they are reported, it may or may not be investigated; if investigated by the PDE, (Pennsylvania Department of Education) they may get a legal slap on the wrist but will probably not be dismissed. However, if a teacher violates these codes, they will most likely be dismissed. This, unfortunately for me, was the general consensus—a result of the knowledge I had gained from contacting numerous lawyers during the summer of 2004.

I feel that Brenda Craiger had violated code # 237.7: Cruelty. According to the PDE (Pennsylvania Department of Education) definition, cruelty was defined as "the intentional, malicious, and unnecessary infliction of physical or psychological pain upon living creatures, particularly human beings." Brenda Craiger intentionally inflicted psychological pain upon me throughout the 2003–04 academic year. In November 2003, in Brenda Craiger's office, I reminded her that every time we had talked, I had cried.

There were several occasions in which I was so upset I found it difficult to drive back to B. C. Patanjali Elementary School.

It is important that the date of December 19, 2004, is noted. I did not inform Dr. Marcel Nulldick of my situation (i.e., my unfair schedule) until that time. On the morning of December 19, 2004, I met with Marcel Nulldick at 7:20 AM, before my day at B. C. Patanjali Elementary School began. During this meeting, I showed Marcel Nulldick a copy of Bertha Both's schedule and a copy of my schedule. I explained to him that Bertha had taken advantage of me and given herself a great deal of free time. I also explained that I had no planning time, no lunch break, no bathroom breaks, and insufficient travel time. He listened and asked me how I had gotten a copy of Bertha Both's schedule. I told him our schedules were posted on the bulletin board in Bertha's classroom. As he was asking me this question, I recalled the day that I ran out to copy it. I saw her schedule, I was utterly amazed and outraged at how much free time she had given herself at my expense, I grabbed the schedule and ran to the copier! I had lucked out because Bertha and her sneaky little aide were not in the classroom when I returned. I quickly rehung the infamous schedule back in the same spot! No one ever saw me do this! Later, when I talked of this incident to my friend Mary at B. C. Patanjali Elementary School, she quietly and firmly advised me, " Now, you hang on to that!" I informed her that I certainly would do so!

I feel that Brenda Craiger was reprimanded for her negligence, and I became the victim of her retaliation. After December 19, 2004, Brenda Craiger's conduct became unbearable. Brenda directed me to meet her in her office every Friday, after I had completed my instruction. My instruction ended at 3:20, I would arrive in her office at 3:25, and she would promptly excuse herself for bus duty! How vindictive was that? I hated being alone in her office because the sense of wrongfulness and negativity was so strong—and I knew that I was not the only teacher she had treated this way. I knew this instinctively from the depths of my being. If the walls of Brenda Craiger's office could speak out they would tell the many stories of how she victimized some teachers and significantly favored other teachers! She would return from bus duty and keep me there until almost 5:00 PM every Friday afternoon. This was one hour past my contracted time! I hated the close proximity—the fact that I was alone in her office waiting for her—and the fact that she and I were in her office and no one other than us was present. I hated this feeling! Who wanted to be in close proximity of a person who has a strong desire to hurt and intentionally destroy one's self-esteem? Her goal was the suppression of my professional success. The close proximity to Brenda Craiger made my internal rage blow up until I cried hysterically!

One Friday afternoon my son, David, was involved in a baseball game that I wanted to see. I had previously e-mailed Brenda of the date ahead of time, only requesting that we could end our meeting by 4:30 PM which would at least have allowed me to see the end of David's baseball game. Even ending our scheduled session at 4:30 PM would have taken me thirty minutes beyond my contracted time. On that specific date Brenda kept me until 5:30 PM! This was one and a half hours past my contracted time! As we ended out session, she vindictively stated, "And you wanted to be out of here early today, didn't you?" In her voice I heard the phoniness, vindictiveness, and hatefulness in which she found delight because she knew she intentionally made me miss an event that was important to me! She did this to me to intentionally provoke me! My rage and anger grew, and once again I drove away from Brenda's Craiger's office crying hysterically because she was truly a tyrant! I could only think about how much I hated her, and how could she sleep at night, and that karma must get her back for her spiteful behavior!

I told Diane Ridgedan about this and I also told her that I believed that when one was kind and positive toward others, it returned to one a hundred or thousand fold, and the same thing happened if one was unkind and caused others to have painful experiences, it returned to one a hundred or maybe a thousand fold! Diane replied, "Yes, I know that too—I do know that!"

As the year progressed and I told some of my friends at B. C. Patanjali Elementary School about the unethical treatment I received at Mountclair Elementary School, they eagerly provided names of former employees who also had been mistreated by Brenda Craiger! Diane Ridgedan, the most ethical person whom I have ever meant, also supplied me with a name. Furthermore, the janitors in this very small school district really had a handle on what was going on. I stayed in my B. C. Patanjali Elementary School classroom working very late and therefore became friendly with the janitors. Because it was a small district, custodial responsibilities included working simultaneously in both B. C. Patanjali and Mountclair Elementary school buildings. The janitors always amazed me with their stories of truth about Brenda Craiger! One janitor informed me of an incident in which he observed a teacher changing answers on several student standardized achievement test answer sheets. Another janitor, who was a friend of mine, witnessed a teacher in Brenda's building changing answers, because she knew if her students' standardized test scores were not higher, Brenda would certainly have her fired because she was not one of Brenda's favorites! Another janitor informed me that Dr. James Ryan, the superintendent, confronted him in person and instructed him to stop saying negative things about Brenda Craiger. This janitor also witnessed a Mountclair teacher having a nervous breakdown because Brenda Craiger had treated him the way she treated me. Diane Ridgedan supplied me with the name of this specific teacher. This specific Mountclair teacher left the teaching profession due to the state of emotional adversity that Brenda Craiger had caused him to experience!

I feel that Brenda Craiger has violated code #237.3: immorality. According to the PDE (Pennsylvania Department of Education), the definition of immorality was defined as "conduct which offends the morals of the Commonwealth and is a bad example to the youth whose ideals a professional educator or charter school staff member has a duty to foster and elevate." There are several instances in which teachers made comments to me that proved Brenda Craiger had shared confidential information about my performance with those teachers. For example, I am aware that Brenda Craiger informed a certain teacher that she had requested Dr. Marcel Nulldick to dismiss me midyear. Brenda Craiger described me as a teacher who was not "permanent." A *student* informed me of this conversation. One of two things happened: Brenda Craiger told a certain group of teachers that I was not "permanent" and those teachers talked about it in front of a student, or Brenda Craiger told those teachers I was not "permanent" in front of a student. I never shared any personal information with Mountclair employees, however they knew that I was not "permanent," that I had used some of my sick days, that I was not allowed to use the same set of reading books in both buildings, that Brenda Craiger wanted to have me dismissed, and that I had a specific meeting time with Brenda Craiger each Friday (from 4:00 PM to 5:00 PM). I *never* spoke to anyone in the Mountclair building regarding these issues, and Brenda Craiger was the only Mountclair employee who knew these confidential facts. I have documented dates and comments made to me regarding Brenda Craiger's defiance of confidentiality. Furthermore, Brenda Craiger violated my teacher contract because she was not allowed to keep me one hour past my contractual time. She did this to me on a weekly basis for several consecutive months.

I feel that Brenda Craiger also violated code # 235.4: Practices.

The PDE (Pennsylvania Department of Education) defined Practices as "behaviors and attitudes that are based on a set of values that the professional education community believes and accepts. These values are evidenced by the professional educator's conduct toward students and colleagues, and the educator's employer and community. When teacher candidates become professional educators in this Commonwealth, they are expected to abide by this section." On May 28, 2004, I was in the building of Mountclair during the morning hours due to meetings. I walked in and heard Brenda Craiger saying my name to Bertha Both. The paper scheduling my dismissal of June 2, 2004, with Dr. Marcel Nulldick was turned face down on the table in the room where Brenda Craiger and Bertha Both were talking. Brenda Craiger had no right to discuss my dismissal (or any other confidential information) with Bertha Both. Therefore, Brenda Craiger violated my fundamental rights of dignity, privacy, and respect.

I informed Dr. Marcel Nulldick of the incident when a student felt he did not have to obey my classroom rules because I was "different" and I was not "permanent." I submitted detailed documentation explaining this incident to Dr. Marcel Nulldick. After he read my documentation, he informed me that if others were behaving in an unprofessional manner, I should have gone directly to Brenda Craiger, the building administrator! Oh! Great advice from the assistant superintendent! I tried not to laugh when he made such a ridiculous statement! So, Should I have informed Brenda Craiger that she was the cause of this unprofessional behavior? Should I have informed her that she was behaving in an unprofessional manner when she shared confidential information about me with other teachers and possibly some students? Great advice! Brenda Craiger was the last person I would speak to—I would ONLY meet with her when I was directed to do so. I hated being in her energy field—her aura was yellow and brown because she had victimized many people. I wouldn't be surprised if she suffered through negative experiences in her life because I believed in karma. If this happens to her, she brought it upon herself! I really felt sympathy for her because if she was hurting me, she was also hurting herself!

I feel that Brenda Craiger has violated code #235.11: Professional Relationships. According to the PDE (Pennsylvania Department of Education) definition Professional Relationships is as follows: "The professional educator may not: (1) Knowingly and intentionally deny or impede a colleague in the exercise or enjoyment of a professional right or privilege in being an educator. (2) Knowingly and intentionally distort evaluations of colleagues. (3) Sexually harass a fellow employee. (4) Use coercive means or promise special treatment to influence professional decisions of colleagues." I feel that Brenda Craiger has intentionally distorted my evaluations due to the fact that Dr. Marcel Nulldick reprimanded her because she was not present when Bertha Both assigned my caseload. During the 2003–2004 academic year, Brenda Craiger observed me three times; her observations were either "unsatisfactory" or "marginal." These observations have impeded me from obtaining a position in another school district. I was not able to supply "satisfactory" observations from the spring semester. However, my fall observation/evaluation, completed by Bill Bellkoe, the principal of B. C. Patanjali Elementary School, is "satisfactory". As the year continued, I became more and more proficient! I did *not* get worse with practice!

I feel that Brenda Craiger has violated code #235.4: Practices. According to the PDE (Pennsylvania Department of Education) definition Practices are defined as follows: "Professional practices are behaviors and attitudes that are based on a set of values that the professional education community believes and accepts. These values are evidenced by the professional educator's conduct toward students and colleagues, and the educator's employer and community. When teacher candidates become professional educators in this Commonwealth, they are expected to abide by this section." Brenda Craiger was inconsistent and unfair in her treatment of me. She has earned the reputation of running a school of favorites. I feel that Brenda Craiger was an unfair supervisor because she allowed Bertha Both to have ample planning time at my expense. I had no planning time at B. C. Patanjali or at Mountclair. According to my contract, I was also fifteen to twenty minutes short per day of designated travel time. The union representative at B. C. Patanjali Elementary School looked over my schedule more than one time and informed me of this contractual violation! When I spoke to Brenda Craiger about my unfair schedule, she told me to talk to Dr. Lurk or Dr. Marcel Nulldick.

I feel that Brenda Craiger has violated code #237.8: Negligence. I feel Brenda Craiger was negligent when she allowed the unfair scheduling and the actions categorized as acts of cruelty to occur in her building. Brenda Craiger allowed another teacher, Bertha Both, to designate my schedule. When Bertha Both took advantage of me, Brenda Craiger did nothing to remedy the situation. Bertha Both gave herself ample planning time at my expense. I have documented a copy of my afternoon schedule and a copy of Bertha Both's afternoon schedule. It was Brenda Craiger's duty to be present during scheduling, and it was Brenda Craiger's duty to ensure that both special education teachers had a planning period, a lunch period, and a progress monitoring period.

I feel that Brenda Craiger has violated code #237.9: Crimes involving moral turpitude. On Friday, January 16, 2004, Brenda Craiger handed me a letter depicting negative aspects of my performance. I was alone in her office when she handed me the letter. She was extremely rude to me. Her tones were rude, and she informed me that this letter would hurt my midyear evaluation. I was not aware of the fact that I could have asked for a union representative to accompany me. This letter was disconcerting and I was so distraught I could barely drive, after leaving Mountclair, to return to B. C. Patanjali. I feel that she was actually happy to hand me such a negative letter. I drove away from Mountclair on 1/16/04 well aware of the fact that Brenda Craiger was going to do everything in her power to have me dismissed from the Souless Area School District. Brenda Craiger had a reputation for becoming obsessed with vendettas, and she did not let up until that person resigned, was dismissed, or had a nervous breakdown. I have a list of names of teachers Brenda Craiger has forced out of the school district. One teacher had a nervous breakdown, and I spoke to another Souless Area School District employee who witnessed this nervous breakdown. Another teacher was forced into early retirement due to the conduct of Brenda Craiger. Two other teachers left the district due to their relationship with Brenda Craiger. If this situation and documentation were to go into litigation, those teachers could be subpoenaed because the conduct of Brenda Craiger needs to be legally addressed. I feel that Brenda Craiger should have a class action suit against her and then be dismissed from her position because she certainly has violated every misconduct code in existence!

I feel that Brenda Craiger has violated code #235.11: Professional Relationships. I feel that Brenda Craiger knowingly and intentionally distorted information in her letter of January 16, 2004. It was a letter of lies and distortion. Surprise! Surprise! I felt this letter was nothing more than Brenda Craiger's retaliation against me due to her negligence, which was apparent when Dr. Marcel Nulldick compared my schedule to Bertha Both 's schedule.

I feel that Brenda Craiger violated code # 235.11 Professional Relationships when she intentionally distorted my evaluation. I feel that Brenda Craiger violated code #237.9: Crimes involving moral turpitude.

On February 11, 2004, Brenda Craiger observed me. On February 13, 2004, at the district office in Dr. James Ryan's office, Brenda Craiger and I had our post-observation conference. I was once again alone in an office with Brenda Craiger. There was a different atmosphere in Dr. James Ryan's office because he was a man of kindness and integrity, however Brenda Craiger's behavior remained consistent. Brenda Craiger's vile behavior overwhelmed me. She was rude, her tones were sharp, and I felt she was happy to hand me an "unsatisfactory" evaluation. My students were well behaved during the observation. Brenda Craiger handed me the unsatisfactory observation and commented, "I am sure this is *not* what you were expecting." I saw through her phoniness! In fact, it was exactly what I had expected from her! Of course she would give me a terrible evaluation—even if I were the most perfect, proficient, master teacher in the world, she would have said negative things about me! She had a vendetta against me, and her way of retaliation was through her power to give me a negative evaluation. Ironically, I had earned a proficient and satisfactory evaluation when Bill Bellkoe formally observed me in October. Similarly, when Dr. Lurk observed me in November, she had many positive comments regarding my classroom performance, but she never bothered to write up the formal observation on the required document. Brenda Craiger knew that it was *not* what I deserved. She reminded me that I would be working with her only through June. I was very emotional when I drove home from the district office that day. I was thinking about being dismissed and how this unsatisfactory evaluation would impede me from ever getting hired in another school district. I almost had a car accident at an intersection where a tractor trailer was driving in my direction. I was really too upset to drive; but I had no choice.

During the following week, I informed Bill Bellkoe of my experience with Brenda Craiger. I stated, "I hope Dr. Marcel Nulldick is intelligent enough to see through Brenda Craiger's lies."

Bill Bellkoe replied, "Yes, he is intelligent enough to see through Bev's lies. But you must remember, no matter what happens, Marcel Nulldick must take the word of his principal over the word of his teacher." I informed Bill about some of the distorted facts that Brenda Craiger had written regarding my performance. I also informed Bill Bellkoe that Brenda Craiger hated me. He replied, "Well, she hates me too!"

I routinely left Mountclair at 4:00 PM and returned to B. C. Patanjali. I stayed in the Mountclair building **not** one second past the time that I had been directed to do so! Many days I returned to B. C. Patanjali in tears.

My friends in this building consoled me numerous times. Brenda Craiger had formerly held the position of principal at B. C. Patanjali Elementary School. Ironically enough, the four names of teachers, which I feel need to be subpoenaed in the opportunity of litigation, were given to me by four different Souless Area School District employees. The inappropriate conduct of Brenda Craiger needs to be legally addressed. I feel she should be legally dismissed from her professional position based on the outcome of a class action suit!

Brenda Craiger violated code 237.9: Crimes involving moral turpitude. Here is the PDE (Pennsylvania Department of Education) definition of crimes involving moral turpitude.

(1) That element of personal misconduct in the private and social duties which a person owes to his fellow human beings or to society in general, which characterizes the act done as an act of baseness, vileness, or depravity, and contrary to the accepted and customary rule of right and duty between two human beings.

(2) Conduct done knowingly contrary to justice, honesty or good morals.

(3) Intentional, knowing or reckless conduct causing bodily injury to another or intentional, knowing or reckless conduct which, by physical menace, puts another in fear of imminent serious bodily injury.

Brenda Craiger's vileness was present even prior to December 19, 2004. Early in November 2003, when I had had exactly two months of teaching experience, Brenda Craiger used rude and harsh tones and made the following statement: "You are incapable of making professional decisions." The internal rage and anger grew! I wanted to call her many unprofessional names—but I did not! I wanted to call her a bitch! I was so upset that I could not drive back to B. C. Patanjali that day. Brenda Craiger's vileness existed throughout the 2003–2004 academic year. My colleagues from B. C. Patanjali informed me that this hatred directed from Brenda Craiger toward me was the result of a long-term animosity between Brenda Craiger and Bill Bellkoe. My colleagues informed me that I was Brenda Craiger's victim of retaliation against Bill Bellkoe. They described this animosity between the two principals as Brenda Craiger's reason for treating me with an extreme amount of vileness throughout the 2003-2004 academic year. This animosity would explain why she treated me with cruelty, but it does not explain why she treated many other teachers with hostility. In addition to this existing animosity, Brenda Craiger was well known for her history of harshness and unethical treatment of numerous teachers. These two facts combined, created a professional situation of adversity for me—Brenda Craiger was not going to let me win. Furthermore, the animosity does not explain why she had chosen favorites in her building. Certainly, the animosity does not excuse her from her heinous behaviors and acts of cruelty. Brenda Craiger was not invited to my August 2003 interview. However, several other Souless Area School District principals were present.

I feel that Brenda Craiger also violated code # 235.4: Practices. On May 14, 2004, I was accused of not providing instruction to my Mountclair children. On this day, the fifth grade children had a field trip. I was responsible for eleven Mountclair children, eight of whom were fifth graders. They were *not* in the building for me to instruct. Therefore I entered Mountclair later than usual. I used my identification swipe card to enter the building; I can *prove* that I was in the building on May 14, 2004. The three children who did not attend the May 14 field trip were students in Shannon Mackely's fourth grade classroom.

When I explained to Shannon Mackely that I would complete *Explode The Code* lessons to these remaining three children, she replied, "It is fine with me if you want to do it that way." It was not possible to continue with a scripted reading lesson when eight of my students were out of the building due to a field trip. I contacted Shannon Mackely to make sure I was not interrupting anything in the regular education classroom. I worked with those three students for one hour and fifteen minutes on May 14. According to the IEPs of each of these children, I was only required to instruct these children thirty-five minutes per day. However, the *Explode the Code* lessons were completed because they were part of the curriculum required by the IEP goals of these children. Significantly, I can prove through the use of my swipe card, and my documentation of the conversation with Shannon Mackely, that I fulfilled my responsibilities as special education teacher on May 14, 2004. The fact that Brenda Craiger held the circumstances of May 14, 2004, against me was a distortion of facts.

I feel that Brenda Craiger violated code # 237.7: Cruelty. Brenda Craiger intentionally kept me one hour past my contracted time each Friday. Brenda Craiger and I had a routinely scheduled meeting time: every Friday at 3:40 PM in Brenda Craiger's office. Each Friday I would arrive as quickly as possible. Upon my arrival, Brenda Craiger would promptly and vindictively excuse herself, informing me that she must remain outside the building during bus duty. I sat alone, waiting inside Brenda Craiger's office until she returned at 4:00 PM. Brenda Craiger kept me until almost 5:00 PM each Friday, always going forty-five minutes to one hour over my contracted time. I felt that this scenario of bus duty and late Friday meetings was a spiteful and vile arrangement.

Early one Friday afternoon my son, David, was involved in a baseball game that I wanted to see. I had previously e-mailed Brenda of the date ahead of time, only requesting that we could end our meeting my by 4:30 PM which would at least have allowed me to see the end of David's baseball game. Brenda Craiger replied to that e-mail and informed me that we would try to "speed things up." As usual, our meeting began with her bus dismissal and my waiting alone in her office. On this day she kept me later than ever. Even ending our scheduled session at 4:30 PM would have taken me thirty minutes beyond my contracted time. On that specific date Brenda kept me later than usual, until 5:30 PM! This was one and a half hours past my contracted time! As we ended our session, she vindictively stated, "And you wanted to be leave early today, didn't you?" In her sarcastic voice I heard the phoniness, vindictiveness, and hatefulness in which she found delight because she knew she intentionally made me miss an event that was important to me! She did this to me to intentionally provoke me! My rage and anger grew, and once again I drove away from Brenda's Craiger's office crying hysterically because she was truly a tyrant! Why did she want to torture me? I could only think about how much I hated her, and how could she sleep at night, and that karma must get her back for her spiteful behavior!

She was evil to the core! The sound of her voice producing this statement of phoniness made the rage and anger inside me rise! Brenda Craiger did this to me out of spite!

I feel this is one more instance in which Brenda Craiger violated code # 237.9: Crimes involving moral turpitude. Certainly this was an act of baseness and spitefulness. I feel she was sarcastic, rude, and spiteful. It was 5:30 PM when I finally got into my car. Every Friday I left the building crying because Brenda Craiger was extremely rude to me whenever Dr. Marcel Nulldick was not present. I was not aware at that time that as a union member, I could have requested a union representative to accompany me during my Friday meetings with Brenda Craiger. One of the union representatives—or at least the president of the union, or any building representative—could have informed me not to attend any meetings without union member representation.

I feel that Brenda Craiger has violated code # 235.11, Professional Relationships, when she intentionally distorted my lesson plans. I feel Brenda Craiger did everything she could possibly do to have me dismissed. I feel that Brenda Craiger's intentions behind ITAP (the Intensive Teacher Assistance Program) was to look at me intensively so she could find grounds for my dismissal. I feel Brenda Craiger falsified information, especially regarding my lesson plans and my evaluations. It was necessary for Brenda Craiger to falsify information regarding my performance because all of my work was satisfactory and proficient. If this situation goes into litigation, I need a reading specialist to examine the fact that Brenda Craiger wanted me to cover one lesson per day. This shows a lack of knowledge about how special education children learn and a lack of knowledge of how Reading Mastery should be presented.

The intensity of my negative feelings toward Brenda Craiger grew beyond any emotional adversity or level of emotional turmoil that I had ever experienced. Whenever anyone in my household would behave in a negative or mean manner, I would reply, "Now that's a Brenda Craiger!"

Reading Specialist

On October 30, 2004, Jone Castle, an employee from the local Intermediate Unit, who trained the teachers to instruct Reading Mastery, came to observe me at Mountclair. Jone Castle questioned the fact that I had been taking home the comprehension section of Reading Mastery for grading purposes. I informed Jone Castle that I graded this segment of Reading Mastery at home to speed up the process. I was well aware of the fact that Brenda Craiger wanted me to cover one lesson per day per group. I informed Jone Castle of Brenda Craiger's expectations. Jone Castle stated that the children needed to have instant feedback on the comprehension questions.

I attempted to explain this to Brenda Craiger throughout the 2003–2004 academic year, indicating that the children would make statements such as, "Mrs. Hall, you're going too fast!" Regardless of these details, Brenda Craiger, even in May of 2004, told me to list one Reading Mastery lesson per day on my lesson plans. I informed Brenda Craiger that this was *not* reasonable and that I could not cover one lesson per day because the textbooks were becoming too difficult for some of my special education children.

I spoke to Diane Ridgedan about this situation, and she replied, "What does the word *mastery* mean?" Brenda Craiger told me to list one reading lesson per day in my lesson plans even though I could not cover them. She directed me, "This is how I want you to write your lesson plans, even if you can't cover one lesson per day." As she stated this, I sensed the wrongfulness, and my instincts told me she was creating one more twisted element of sabotage on my behalf!

During the ITAP meeting of May 18, 2004, Brenda Craiger announced that she had "a concern" regarding the lesson plans that I turned in. She announced to the ITAP team that although my lesson plans had stated that I would cover one lesson per day, in reality I had only covered three lessons per week. Brenda had a true concern? That liar! I knew she was up to something heinous when she told me, while I was alone with her in her office, to list one lesson per day—even though she and I knew that was not possible. I instinctively was aware that she would use my lesson plans to intentionally distort facts. And she did! The key point here was that the PSEA (Pennsylvania State Education Association) Union Representatives should have instructed me to never meet alone with Brenda Craiger! I was new to the public school system, and the PSEA Union Representatives should have helped me! The fact is that the PSEA Union Representatives also failed me significantly! I paid my union dues that year for nothing—they should have been refunded to me. It was not possible to complete one lesson per day due to time limitations, plus the fact that the learning disabled children were dealing with lessons that were more difficult and lengthy than those that we had covered in September and October of 2003. Once again, in self-defense, I documented the truth and submitted it Dr. Marcel Nulldick. Of course, attached to this letter were my copies of my lesson plans (both before and after the meeting) to prove and defend myself as usual!

5/19/2004
Re: Response To ITAP Meeting of 5/18/2004
Dear Dr. Nulldick,

During our meeting of 5/18/04, Mrs. Craiger announced that I had listed one lesson per day on my Reading Mastery Lesson Plans. Previously, I had handed in lesson plans listing one lesson per day in my plans. I had informed Mrs. Craiger that my reason for having listed only three or four lessons per week was due to the fact that this was actually what I was able to cover. I informed Mrs. Craiger that I was not able to cover five lessons—therefore I changed my plans, even though I knew it was unrealistic to move so quickly.

Following this Friday meeting of 3/5/2004, when I was kept at Mountclair Elementary School until 4:45 pm, my lesson plans have

listed one lesson per day. I made this change on my lesson plans at the request of Mrs. Craiger.
Sincerely,

Katrina Hall
Cc:
Shelly Mitchel
Diane Ridgedan
Brenda Craiger

Look at the time and the energy I spent each day defending myself from the lies of Brenda Craiger! I was innocent! Look at the collective amount of negative energy dispersed through the actions of one tyrant, Brenda Craiger! Why? I will never understand why so much negative energy was dispersed in my defense against Brenda Craiger. After all, she was an administrator in a public school, therefore, she had the power to help people produce positive energy that could have helped the students to learn more, or energy that could have helped new teachers become better teachers. But our time was always wasted in self-defense. Instead of using her administrative power to hurt and victimize, she could have helped many people. I have a great deal of sympathy for Brenda Craiger because she was also hurting herself in many ways.

I had discussed my reading lesson plans with Jone Castle, Diane Ridgedan, and two reading specialists in my building at B. C. Patanjali Elementary School. Each of the four professionals were seasoned and had many years of experience under their belt. They unanimously agreed that it would be beneficial for all the students and for me to use the same reading materials in both elementary buildings. They also unanimously agreed that if I must use Reading Mastery, I should **not** move on to the next lesson until those skills from the previous lesson were mastered; hence "reading mastery." I enjoyed my reading lessons at B. C. Patanjali Elementary School and felt that the children were actually learning more. When I confronted Brenda Craiger, she became rude and angry and informed me that I must continue to use the scripted reading materials in her building. I talked with Bill Bellkoe and showed him the materials that I had been directed to use at Mountclair. Bill was flabbergasted! He was also a certified Reading Specialist and informed me that there was no way he would allow any of his teachers to use a scripted reading program in his building. He felt that it was a disgrace. Brenda Craiger had had no background in teaching reading, and she certainly had not earned her certificate required to be a Reading Specialist! Once again, I was forced to complete seven different reading lesson plans per day—because I had been directed not to use the same reading materials in both buildings! I told Diane Ridgedan, and she just shook her head! Once again she informed me that I was the target of retaliation between two administrators who shared a lifelong professional animosity!

One reason I was dismissed, according to the documentation I received on June 2, 2004, was the fact that I was not able to complete one reading lesson per day with my Mountclair children. This is ludicrous! I feel that this is an example of falsifying information to use against me—Brenda Craiger needed reasons to request my dismissal; when she had none, she created them through falsifying information regarding my lesson plans. During my final ITAP meeting, I mentioned the fact that during the month of May, 2004, I had not seen many of my reading groups due to end-of-the-year activities. I had enclosed the May and June activity sheet—once again, as documentation in my defense for Dr. Marcel Nulldick to read. It was impossible to continue to use scripted reading lessons during the last few weeks of school. During the month of May, I rarely saw my fifth grade students due to field trips, plays, and many other scheduled activities. During the last eight days of school, I did not see any of my fifth grade Mountclair students due to elementary school graduation activities. The fifth grade Mountclair teachers with whom I worked can attest to this fact.

Self-Defense:
Lack Of Communication

Throughout the 2003–2004 academic year, Brenda Craiger's practice of informing Dr. Marcel Nulldick of a problem continued. I was blamed for the lack of communication between Brenda Craiger and myself, when in fact Brenda Craiger would inform Dr. Marcel Nulldick of a problem rather than talking to me. I would learn about her expectations through another source—she never really told me what she expected or exactly what she wanted me to change. I told Diane Ridgedan that I never really knew what Brenda Craiger wanted. Diane, who had thirty years of teaching experience, agreed that she too did not know what Brenda Craiger wanted from me. In retrospect, I do know what she wanted—she wanted me fired—and she achieved this through false documentation! I feel that she had a vendetta against me and that no matter what I did, she would have negative things to say. Dr. Marcel Nulldick had informed me early on that I would be dismissed at the end of the academic year. Therefore, all observation/evaluations from Brenda had to be unsatisfactory! However, I felt obligated to defend myself against the behavior of the tyrant, Brenda Craiger. On May 17, 2004, I wrote the following letter in self-defense. I submitted it to the pertinent group of administrators after Diane Ridgedan proofread it and assisted me in making a few changes in the documentation of defense.

5/14/04
Re: Response To ITAP Team
Dear Dr. Nulldick,

I have been blamed for lack of communication between Mrs. Craiger and myself. On three different occasions I had confronted Mrs. Craiger with my "unfair schedule." She shrugged off my statements and informed me that I should work out my schedule with Dr. Lurk. These three attempts to communicate with Mrs. Craiger were prior to our meeting of January 13, 2004. Two of these attempts were verbal; the third was in writing, in which I had used the words "unfair schedule."

Only one time had Mrs. Craiger communicated any concerns to me. I never knew what she wanted. Only one time had Mrs. Craiger asked me to come into her office to talk about how I should change things or correct things. It was only through communication with you that I discovered Mrs. Craiger was dissatisfied with my work. On the other hand, I have always known what Bill expected. When things were not as he wanted, he directly and immediately told me what he expected. One day during the third marking period, Bill informed me, "That is what I like about you: I tell you to do something and you do it." This is the reason Bill and I have gotten along so well. As a new teacher, I needed to know exactly what my principal wanted. B. C. Patanjali has been the only part of my job where I have had clear expectations and guidelines. Mrs. Craiger never gave me any direction. Without clear direction, how could I begin to do things the way she wanted them completed?

During my discussion with Mrs. Craiger (which took place in early December 2003), she told me to include Language Arts activities. She also told me that I should refer to my groups as "Language Arts groups, not Reading Groups." At that time I retyped my schedule and referred to it as "Language Arts Group A, B, and C". During our meeting of January 13, 2004, Mrs. Craiger complained because I referred to the groups as Language Arts and not Reading Groups. I reminded Mrs. Craiger that I had changed it because she had requested me to do so.

As I went through my academic year, I realized the need to group my B. C. Patanjali children according to reading levels. Several things prevented me from doing so. First, my limited amount of instruction time at B. C. Patanjali made it difficult because my children are reading at the following grade levels: PP1, PP3, 1.0, 2.5, 3.5, 4.5.

Dr. Lurk never gave me a copy of my homebound student's updated IEP. When I requested a copy, I was given an IU phone number. I had made arrangements to meet the OT (Occupational Therapist), early in

September, at the student's place of residence. The OT never showed up at that time. I had contacted my homebound student's former teacher and asked him which activities he had completed with this student. I continued to do what his former teacher had advised. Several weeks later, I asked the OT for a copy of the student's updated IEP, and she supplied it. Her advice to me was, "You must decide what you feel is purposeful." On a daily basis, from B. C. Patanjali Elementary School, I telephoned the student's residence to confirm my attendance on that day. On numerous occasions Mrs. Bergwise, the student's mother, would reply, "He will probably sleep the entire time you are here, but come anyhow." Three weeks before Mike's IEP meeting, the OT shared my session with me at the Bergwise residence. This was in February, not September.

I have attached my letter of 11/24/03. I was NOT the special education teacher who allowed Mindy Rissmiller's IEP to expire. Bertha Both allowed this IEP to expire, and I was blamed for it. Mindy Rissmiller had relocated within the Souless Area School District and therefore came to me with an expired IEP.
Sincerely,

Katrina Hall
Cc:
Dr. James Ryan
Shelly Mitchel
Diane Ridgedan
Brenda Craiger

I feel Brenda Craiger violated code #235.4: Practices, Category #4. Category 4 states that "Professional educators shall exhibit consistent and equitable treatment of students, fellow educators and parents." Brenda Craiger did not treat me with the same respect she had treated her group of favorite teachers. I feel that Brenda Craiger has violated category 4 because she did not exhibit consistent and equitable treatment of Bertha Both and me. In September, 2003, Brenda Craiger told me to retype my schedule and to refer to the Reading Groups as Language Arts Groups, and I did so. I retyped my schedule, referring to the groups as Language Arts groups. The following week she told me to retype the schedule and refer to the groups as Reading/Language Arts Groups. Once again, I retyped the schedule. In the presence of Dr. Marcel Nulldick during a

January meeting, Brenda Craiger told Dr. Marcel Nulldick that I should refer to my groups as "Reading Groups" not "Language Arts Groups".

I reminded Brenda Craiger, in the presence of Dr. Marcel Nulldick, that I had referred to the groups as "Language Arts Groups" because she had instructed me to do so. I reminded Brenda Craiger that I had originally referred to them as Reading Groups. I informed Brenda Craiger: "I changed the title of the groups because you told me to do so—don't you remember?" Brenda Craiger did not answer me. Finally, I retyped the schedule for the third time and referred to them as "Reading Groups," exactly as I had in September of 2003. This is a perfect example of the behavior/conduct of Brenda Craiger. The directives that I received from Brenda Craiger were incongruent. She would instruct me to do something, and then in the presence of Dr. Marcel Nulldick, the Assistant Superintendent, she would turn it against me. During this meeting Dr. Marcel Nulldick became irritated with Brenda Craiger—I could hear it in his voice and was happy that he too was frustrated with her. When the tone of his voice sounded irritated, I tried not to smile. Dr. Marcel Nulldick sighed a lot during that meeting because he was irritated with her! Bill Bellkoe left the room that day because he did not want to see me cry. If Bill Bellkoe had stayed in the conference room that day, he would have certainly enjoyed the frustration in Marcel Nulldick's voice when he spoke to Brenda Craiger!

Brenda Craiger was known for her heinous acts and infamous reputation—she had her favorite teachers, and that was that. Brenda Craiger's common practice of directing me to do something, confirming verbally that I had completed this directive, and then denying the directive in front of Dr. Marcel Nulldick was endless. The sabotage and undermining was consistent throughout the 2003–2004 academic year. Furthermore, the things Brenda Craiger instructed me to do were *not* things that helped me become a better teacher, and neither were they things that would help the children learn more.

I feel that Brenda Craiger has violated code #235.4: Practices. Category 7 states, "Professional educators shall exhibit acceptable and professional language and communication skills. Their verbal and written communication with parents, students, and staff shall reflect sensitivity to the fundamental human rights of dignity, privacy, and respect." Category 8 states that "Professional educators shall be open-minded, knowledgeable and use appropriate judgment and communication skills when responding to an issue within the educational environment." I feel that Brenda Craiger violated categories 7 and 8 when she documented the fact that my data collection was incomplete. Not only did she falsify information, but she also had her secretary, Lucy, make copies of this complete data collection. In January 2004, Brenda Craiger instructed me to complete a data collection on my eleven Mountclair children. She documented that I only provided a data collection for seven of my students. This is false documentation. It took me *only* three school/working days to complete this data collect for each of my eleven Mountclair students. When completed, I personally handed this information to Brenda Craiger, placing it in a yellow pocket folder. I certainly kept a copy of these documents for my personal records. The folder contained three sets of documents, one for each reading group. She had her secretary, Lucy, copy my detailed data collection. If this situation were to result in litigation, I can prove that I had a complete (not incomplete) data collection. Currently, I have the yellow folder in my possession. Brenda Craiger's secretary was underhanded, just like Brenda, and I instinctively knew that Brenda had told her secretary negative things about me.

I feel Brenda Craiger violated code #235.4: Practices, Category #4. Category 4 states that "Professional educators shall exhibit consistent and equitable treatment of students, fellow educators and parents." Brenda Craiger did not treat me with the same respect she had treated Gracie Ling, who had previously used Reading Mastery in her building. This is one more example of how Brenda Craiger has proven to be an unfair administrator. She was unfair to me in many ways. During the previous academic year, Gracie Ling taught Reading Mastery in Brenda Craiger's building. Her lesson plans were simple and Brenda Craiger accepted them. (I attached an example of Gracie Ling's acceptable Reading Mastery lesson plans to my letter of defense for Dr. Marcel Nulldick to view). My lesson plans, in comparison, became more and more detailed—at the request of Brenda Craiger. For example, she requested a listing of page numbers per day, which I provided. How ridiculous and time consuming was that? I told Diane Ridgedan this, and she just shook her head. I considered this directive ludicrous, however I supplied the page numbers, as well as a list of teaching procedures, to my daily lesson plans.

At one point Brenda Craiger told me go on the school website and view the Mountclair agenda on a daily basis. I asked why, and she replied, "Because then you will know what is going on here." Once again, this was not something that helped me become a better teacher or helped the students to learn more. Brenda Craiger has two sets of standards: one set for her favorite teachers and one set for everyone else. In many ways Brenda Craiger was unfair in her overall treatment of me.

I feel that Brenda Craiger violated code #235.4: Practices. In February, 2004, I was absent due to an illness. I had a physician's excuse for this absence. I found out later that Brenda Craiger had discussed my absence with a few of her favorite teachers. Brenda Craiger violated my right to privacy when she discussed my sick days with others.

One day Brenda Craiger accused me of not leaving lesson plans for the substitute. Certainly I had prepared and supplied lesson plans. When I returned after this excused absence, I talked with Brenda Craiger about my substitute plans. She asked me to return to Bertha Both's classroom and get them. I did as requested and handed the lesson plans to Brenda Craiger. They were in a blue folder. Brenda Craiger barely looked at them for one second—she simply thumbed through the outside of the folder—and then she replied, "Okay, so you did them, but they are inadequate; I am going to tell Dr. Marcel Nulldick that your substitute plans are inadequate!" My substitute plans were detailed and well written. If this scenario went into litigation, I would have presented that blue folder in my possession as evidence that I certainly supplied detailed and well written substitute plans during my excused absence. Brenda Craiger describing my substitute plans as inadequate and my not providing plans are two different things. However, Brenda Craiger has documented that I failed to provide lesson plans. Brenda Craiger has falsified information.

It is my belief that my relationship with Brenda Craiger was the reason for my termination. To support this belief, I am reminded of the conversation I had with Dr. Marcel Nulldick earlier in the school year, in which he stated, "What you need is a rapport [with Brenda Craiger]; you have that here [at B. C. Patanjali, with Bill Bellkoe". Each day when I worked in Mountclair, I felt sabotaged and framed. I felt I had a principal who enlisted a certain set of favorite teachers to work against me.

I feel that Brenda Craiger has violated code # 235.11: Professional Relationships. According to the PDE (Pennsylvania Department Of Education) definition Professional Relationships are is defined as follows: "The professional educator may not: (1) Knowingly and intentionally deny or impede a colleague in the exercise or enjoyment of a professional right or privilege in being an educator. (2) Knowingly and intentionally distort evaluations of colleagues. (3) Sexually harass a fellow employee. (4) Use coercive means or promise special treatment to influence professional decisions of colleagues." I feel that Brenda Craiger has intentionally distorted my evaluations. Brenda Craiger intentionally distorted my evaluation of April 15, 2004. I have documentation with the following subject line: "Inaccurate Comparison of Writing Samples." Brenda Craiger used a writing sample from the regular education classroom to support my distorted evaluation of April 15, 2004. The assignment in the regular education classroom was prepared for a contest. The students were given four thirty-five-minute sessions to write their best possible essay for a contest. The completed essay for the writing assignment was spread out over four classes, with a great deal of assistance available. The children had four (or possibly five) adults in the room during these four writing sessions. The children were given help editing and rewriting. During my observation of April 15, 2004, my children had seven minutes to develop one paragraph. The fact that Brenda Craiger made this inaccurate comparison is proof that she has distorted my evaluation of May 3, 2004. Following this unethical incident, I provided written documentation to Dr. Marcel Nulldick defending myself, stating the truth in an attempt to disprove Brenda Craiger's sabotage of the day.

Subject: Inaccurate Comparison Of Writing Samples (5/03/2004)

Rhonda's writing sample (from Mrs. Kane's room) has been attached to my observation of 4/15/04. I confronted Mrs. Kane, asking her questions about her instructional procedures for this writing assignment. I talked with Mrs. Kane for two reasons. First, I realized that I could learn from her many years of teaching experience. Secondly, I realized that Rhonda's writing sample, from Mrs. Kane's room, was of higher quality.

Mrs. Kane informed me that she had used four writing blocks—thirty-five minutes each—to accomplish this piece of writing. The children were instructed to edit and rewrite, and to produce their best quality for an essay contest.

Mrs. Kane recently had a student teacher in her room. Most likely Rhonda was in a classroom with a regular education teacher, a student teacher, and an aide. Rhonda was given some assistance with editing.

In comparison, following my instruction/presentation, my reading group was given seven minutes to complete this writing assignment.

Rhonda was upset, almost in tears, when I told her that her topic would be how she spends her Saturdays. I questioned the emotional state of Rhonda during my lesson. Later, I confronted Mrs. Kane and

*informed her that Rhonda was upset. I informed Mrs. Kane that my
children were assigned a topic. Mrs. Kane informed me that Rhonda's
home life is extremely negative, and therefore having Rhonda think
about how she spends her Saturdays would be the reason for Rhonda's
emotional reaction to my writing assignment.*
Fondly,
Katrina Hall

I submitted the above documentation of defense to Dr. Marcel Nulldick
on May 3, 2004. This piece of documentation (along with many others)
was written in vain—a total waste of my time—it changed nothing, I
was getting fired in June 2004, and that was that! I could have been the
pinnacle master teacher—it did not matter. If Brenda Craiger hated me,
I was gone!

Brenda Craiger tortured me! I continually asked why. Why did I have
to suffer for 180 days? Why was Brenda Craiger so determined to torture
me? Dr. Wayne Dyer has said, "Every single person who's drifted in and out
of your life is a part of your Divinely chosen experience. As you move into
the world of inspiration, you'll find it easy—and even necessary—to give
thanks for all of these people, and to take serious note of what they brought
to you." I don't know how I survived the 2003– 2004 academic year. I
had endured previous financial scarcity—this certainly was a motivating
factor. Also, it took human strength beyond recognition and a burning
desire to teach children! Over and over, day after day, I would think, "I
can't do this anymore—not one more day! I'll just quit." I truly loved the
children—it was my emotional connection to my students that kept me
going! Mother Teresa once said, "The important thing is not how much
we accomplish, but how much love we put into our deeds every day." I
loved my students and I loved preparing lesson plans, especially for my B.
C. Patanjali Elementary School students. But still I questioned why God
would allow this to happen to me. Why? Why did God allow this tyrant,
Brenda Craiger, to torture me for 180 days? What lessons did God want
me to learn from this experience? Dr. Wayne W. Dyer has instructed us to
"Anticipate a world at peace. Expect health, abundance, and love in your
life and in the lives of all others. Know that for every act of apparent evil,
there are a million acts of kindness, and that's where you need to focus
your attention."

I feel that Dr. Marcel Nulldick distorted and falsified information
regarding my dismissal from the Souless Area School District. Bill Bellkoe,

Principal, observed me on October 28, 2003. This observation was listed as Satisfactory. However, there is no mention of this observation on my PDE (Pennsylvania Department of Education) 426 form of June 2, 2004. I feel that Dr. Marcel Nulldick has unequivocally impeded my opportunity to work in surrounding school districts. I feel that Dr. Marcel Nulldick has violated code #235.11: Professional Relationships. I feel that Dr. Marcel Nulldick has made discriminatory remarks regarding my professional performance and has therefore impeded my ability to become employed in another school district. I am aware that Dr. Marcel Nulldick was formerly employed with the Iliad Area School District. During August 2004 I was successfully interviewed at the Iliad Area School District. Following the interview, I was introduced to the superintendent as "the candidate." I am aware of the fact that the superintendent (an old friend of Marcel's) contacted Dr. Marcel Nulldick soon after my interview. During August 2004 I was successfully interviewed by Dr. Raymond Beach of the Odyssey Area School District. During the interview, Dr. Raymond Beach informed me that he was a close friend of Dr. Marcel Nulldick and that they attended the same church. Dr. Raymond Beach asked me if I knew Dr. Marcel Nulldick. I simply answered yes. I am aware of the fact that Dr. Beach contacted Dr. Marcel Nulldick by telephone.

I visualized Dr. Marcel Nulldick sitting beside his friend in the church pew, holding his Bible and simultaneously advising Dr. Beach not to hire me. Dr. Marcel Nulldick was a person who would attend church for a show—not because he was a spiritual person. Spiritual people do not attempt to screw someone out of a job! Spiritual people do not assist the Brenda Craigers of the world when they victimize a hard working person! Why? Why did this happen to me? What lesson did God want me to learn from this? Mother Teresa once said, "I see Jesus Christ in His distressing disguise." How could I see any good in this distressing situation?

If this situation had resulted in litigation, I could prove that these telephone conversations had occurred. During August 2004, Shelly Mitchel informed Diane Ridgedan that the telephone calls were coming through, requesting references from Dr. Marcel Nulldick. Certainly I did *not* list his name—but concerning administrators, it is a small world; they all know each other. Diane Ridgedan informed me of these telephone requests for references regarding my potential employment with surrounding school districts. Even though I had not listed Dr. Marcel Nulldick as a reference, he was contacted by several surrounding school districts. I also had a successful interview with the Hatsville Area School District during the month of August 2004. I later learned that a former Hatsville Area School District principal became employed with the Souless Area School District during the summer of 2004. This former Hatsville Area School District principal is currently employed as principal of an elementary school in the Souless Area School District. I felt that I could not apply to these surrounding school districts for the 2005–2006 school year. If Dr. Marcel Nulldick said negative things about me, I would not have the opportunity to even obtain an interview, let alone be hired.

On December 19, 2004, I contacted Dr. Marcel Nulldick regarding my schedule. I presented Dr. Nulldick with a copy of Bertha Both 's schedule and informed him that I had no planning period built into my school day. I informed him that no administrator was present when Bertha Both gave me my afternoon schedule, and that Bertha Both increased my Special Education caseload and decreased her own caseload. I informed Dr. Marcel Nulldick that a homebound student had been placed in the middle of my instruction day. I informed Dr. Marcel Nulldick that I felt Bertha Both had taken advantage of me and that Bertha Both 's schedule was deceitful. Bertha Both had given herself ample planning time at my expense. Dr. Marcel Nulldick informed me that he would look into my schedule and get back to me. I felt that Dr. Marcel Nulldick should have assigned Bertha Both one of my three reading groups, so that I would have had a planning period. Although I explained my situation to Dr. Marcel Nulldick, he *never* changed anything in my schedule.

After December 19, 2004, Dr. Marcel Nulldick reprimanded Brenda Craiger and Bertha Both for taking advantage of me. Before and after this date, they behaved unethically and unprofessionally. I felt that I could not continue to work under these circumstances. I felt that I would have a nervous breakdown if I did not resign. Prior to December 19, 2004, both Bertha Both and Brenda Craiger were rude, cruel, and unprofessional. After December 19, 2004, my situation at Mountclair became unbearable. I cried every day driving to and from the Mountclair building.

I was observed/evaluated by Bill Bellkoe on October 28, 2003. According to Bill Bellkoe, the Principal of B. C. Patanjali Elementary School, my professional performance was satisfactory. As a new teacher, I know that my instruction improved through the passing weeks. However, on the Pennsylvania Department of Education 426 form, there is no mention of my satisfactory evaluation dated October 28, 2003. Therefore, I feel Dr. Marcel Nulldick has violated code #235.11: Professional Relationships. Dr. Marcel Nulldick has intentionally omitted my satisfactory evaluation completed by Bill Bellkoe, on 10/28/03, and has therefore intentionally distorted information used for my dismissal.

On March 25, 2004, Dr. Marcel Nulldick observed/evaluated me at B. C. Patanjali Elementary School. Bill Bellkoe was instructed by Dr. Marcel Nulldick to *not* attend this formal observation. I feel that Dr. Marcel Nulldick has knowingly and intentionally distorted my observation/ evaluation results.

On February 13, 2004, Dr. Marcel Nulldick informed me that I would be dismissed in June. Bill Bellkoe was present during this conversation. After Dr. Marcel Nulldick left the building of B. C. Patanjali Elementary school, Bill Bellkoe and I talked. What I remember most about that day was *not* the fact that I would be fired in June, but the tears in Bill Bellkoe's eyes when he talked with me. Bill advised me, on that day, "Resign—don't get fired!" Later, during the summer of 2004, when Dr. Nulldick was giving me negative references, I had begun payment for legal services through a PSEA lawyer. This lawyer, who took my money and did nothing, had informed me, "It would have been better if you had gotten fired."

Dr. Marcel Nulldick informed me on February 13, 2004, that I would be dismissed in June 2004. Bill Bellkoe was a witness to this conversation. Any formal observation/evaluation completed between February 13, 2004, and June 2, 2004, was evaluated as marginal or unsatisfactory. Because I had been informed of my dismissal, administrators needed to evaluate me as marginal or unsatisfactory, otherwise, there would be no basis for my dismissal of 6/2/04. Dr. Marcel Nulldick had instructed Shelly Mitchel to skew my evaluation—Shelly thought my methods of instruction, my teaching strategies, and my relationship with my students were proficient.

I feel that my instruction and professional performance improved with each passing week. Bill Bellkoe felt I "had many strong qualities" as a teacher. On October 28, 2003, I was evaluated as satisfactory. I feel that any observation after this date is a falsification of information. I feel that Dr. Marcel Nulldick dismissed me for one reason only: my poor relationship with Brenda Craiger.

During the week of April 5–11, 2004, Dr. Marcel Nulldick and I talked. I was very upset during the conversation because I had recently been handed a set of goals for the Mountclair children, which Bertha Both had written in the previous academic year. I already felt overburdened, and I was expected to prepare lesson plans to accomplish each goal for eleven different children. On this day, I asked Dr. Nulldick if he was aware of the fact that Elaine, Bertha Both's student, was frequently ill due to severe health problems; this absence gave Bertha Both another free planning period during each school day. He replied, "I know that." I reminded Dr. Marcel Nulldick of the fact that Bertha Both had given herself an extra planning period when she scheduled Elaine as a one-on-one instructional period. I reminded Dr. Marcel Nulldick that Diane Ridgedan (on 9/5/04) had told Bertha Both not to give me so many students, but Bertha Both did not listen. Dr. Marcel Nulldick replied, "Yes, I know that, and when that teacher [Bertha Both] did that to you, she put a noose around her own neck." Amazing—the Assistant Superintendent made this comment to me in regard to the behavior of another teacher! If this situation had gone into litigation, I wonder if Dr. Marcel Nulldick, Assistant Superintendent, would recall making this statement to me. Or would he just say, "I don't recall making such a statement to Mrs. Hall"? I feel that Dr. Marcel Nulldick was aware of the fact that Bertha Both had taken advantage of me throughout the 2003–2004 school year. When Dr. Marcel Nulldick made this statement to me, he was admitting that I had been treated unfairly at Mountclair. During this meeting, I also mentioned the fact that Brenda Craiger constantly complained about my lesson plans. I handed my plans to Dr. Marcel Nulldick and asked him, "In what ways do these lesson plans **not** meet district requirements?"

He replied, "Each lesson plan should have a teaching procedure." I was too distraught and upset to think clearly; however, the lesson plans in my hand contained a detailed teaching procedure. When I submitted a letter of defense to Dr. Marcel Nulldick, I also enclosed a set of Mountclair lesson plans, which contained teaching procedures. This question took him by surprise—I instinctively knew this! If I had not been emotional during this part of my meeting with Dr. Marcel Nulldick, I would have stated that my Mountclair lesson plans currently contained a daily teaching procedure.

Dr. Marcel Nulldick informed me that if he had been officially assistant superintendent in September 2003, my schedule would have been different. I was aware of the fact that homebound instruction was contracted out for after-school employment. I was aware of the fact that the previous teacher of this same homebound student had been paid to go to the student's home after school each day. Why did Dr. Lurk assign homebound instruction in the middle of my school day? This teacher also told me that if this student slept during his scheduled hour of instruction, he would simply leave the residence. I was also aware of the fact that an administrator should have been present when my schedule and caseload were being determined. Dr. Marcel Nulldick did not officially become assistant superintendent until sometime in November 2003. However, on the PDE (Pennsylvania Department of Education) Form 426, dated June 2, 2004, it is documented that he has completed one year seniority as assistant superintendent with the Souless Area School District.

I feel that I was dismissed based upon falsified information. Furthermore, there are reasons for compliance of caseload limits. When Bertha Both determined my schedule and caseload, my number of special education students well exceeded the legal limit. Therefore, my caseload at Souless Area School District was over the compliance set forth by the Bureau of Special Education.

I was the only special education teacher in the Souless Area School District with no planning, no inclusion, a homebound in the middle of my instructional day, and a caseload that violated special education state regulations. My schedule was brutally intense, and I worked an endless number of hours on my own personal time in an attempt to manage this unfair number of students and the unfair schedule.

I feel that Dr. Marcel Nulldick has falsified information regarding my dismissal and has therefore distorted information contained in the summary of June 2, 2004. Certainly, the use of Tim Bella's IEP is a falsification of documentation. Furthermore, I have in my possession a detailed grade book, which no one ever asked to see. On May 20, 2004, Dr. Marcel Nulldick and I were talking about my situation at Mountclair Elementary School. Dr. Marcel Nulldick mentioned the fact that my professional year at B. C. Patanjali Elementary had gone well. Dr. Marcel Nulldick stated, "It really has clicked here [referring to B. C. Patanjali Elementary] for you!" However on June 2, 2004, Dr. Nulldick contradicted himself. I questioned the fact that there was no mention of Bill Bellkoe's observation in my end–of-the-year summary. Dr. Marcel Nulldick replied, "It would have been different if the problem had been in only one building, but it was in both." This is not true—my work at B. C. Patanjali Elementary School was satisfactory and proficient. I had a rapport with Bill Bellkoe and had earned satisfactory evaluations. On June 2, 2004, Dr. Marcel Nulldick informed me, "I have seen growth, but in May, not in November." The academic year 2003–2004 was my first year of teaching Special Education in a public school.

Dr. Lurk was fired a few days prior to Christmas vacation, I felt empathy for her because she was a kind person, even though she had been very unfair to me. The Supervisor of Special Education was replaced with Shelly Mitchel. Shelly Mitchel had previously worked as a guidance counselor for the Souless Area School District. Shelly had also worked as a special education teacher in an elementary school earlier in her career. With a new supervisor, I felt it imperative that I inform her of my situation—how the tyrant Brenda Craiger had treated me under the supervision of Dr. Lurk. Therefore, on February 9, 2004, I wrote a letter to Dr. Marcel Nulldick and copied Shelly Mitchel. The letter read as follows.

Dear Dr. Marcel Nulldick,

I would like to make you aware of the details of my afternoon assignment. I also feel Shelly Mitchel should be aware of these things. Originally, Dr. Lurk had given me an assignment that excluded Mountclair. She had informed me that I would have B. C. Patanjali Elementary School, plus Mike Bergwise, plus an Adaptive PE class. She also thought my B. C. Patanjali caseload was three, not six, which quickly grew to eight. Before I began with my Adaptive PE class and my work with Mike Bergwise, Dr. Lurk informed me that I would have a math group or a reading group at Mountclair. Furthermore, the B. C. Patanjali Elementary School special education teacher had never before been assigned to Mountclair in the afternoon. Gracie Ling had always worked with Bertha Both.

When I arrived at Mountclair, Bertha Both handed me a schedule that consisted of three reading groups, forty-five minutes each with no breaks between, using Reading Mastery. Bertha Both handed me an intense afternoon schedule and had given herself a math group of one or two children (thirty minutes in length) plus ample planning time. She had also given herself a thirty-minute allotment of time to assist me with Reading Mastery. She never helped me in any way. No administrator was present when Bertha Both determined my afternoon schedule. Diane Ridgedan was present. Diane informed Bertha Both that I should teach only two of her reading groups. Bertha Both replied, "No, because I would have to change around my whole schedule." I feel I have been taken advantage of by Bertha Both.

I talked with Dr. Lurk about the intensity of my schedule. I informed Dr. Lurk that Bertha Both had made each group forty-five minutes in length rather than thirty minutes in length. Dr. Lurk was surprised and not aware of this. Dr. Lurk was not expecting me to do conferences, grades, or progress monitoring for Bertha Both's students.

Dr. Lurk was very surprised when I informed her that Brenda Craiger expected me to be part of Bertha Both's conferences. Gracie Ling had always worked with Bertha Both. Dr. Lurk was not aware of these expectations, because Gracie Ling had not been required to do Bertha Both's conferences, grades, and progress monitoring.

It has been difficult for me to feel connected with Mountclair. For most of my time at Mountclair, I did not have a folder for my lesson plans. Bertha Both told me to put my lesson plans inside her folder. Until recently I did not have a mailbox at Mountclair. On 2/29/04 Brenda put a note in every teacher's mailbox except mine. The note was informing the faculty that Dr. James Ryan, the Superintendent, would be in the building that day.

On 1/08/04 I disciplined a student during my reading group at Mountclair. The student felt that it was not necessary to obey me because I am not a "permanent" teacher. I knew instantly that this student had overheard another teacher at Mountclair talking about me. Many conversations about me have taken place, in a nondiscreet and unprofessional manner, on the other side of the divider.

Another factor that has made this year very difficult is the fact that I am required to use a different set of reading materials in B. C. Patanjali and Mountclair. I am responsible for presenting six reading lessons per day: three at B. C. Patanjali and three at Mountclair. If I had permission to use the same reading materials in both buildings, it would require less preparation time.

Another factor that has made this year very difficult has been my mentor assignment. Kara Keep is in another building, and this has certainly made things inconvenient for she and I. Having another Special Ed teacher working in my home base would have made life significantly easier.

I felt it was unfair to be expected to use Reading Mastery materials without having attended the training sessions at the IU. However, these are the only reading materials I am permitted to use for my Mountclair students.

During our meeting of 1/13/04, you mentioned the importance of communication between Brenda and I. I feel everything I do and say, she is going to turn around and write negative notes to you about me. My words with Brenda will be few and well chosen.

Three weeks before Dr. Lurk was dismissed, she asked me how many children I had at B. C. Patanjali Elementary School. She thought I only had three. I currently have six, and two additional are being tested and will begin instruction with me in the very near future. How could Dr. Lurk not be aware of how heavy my caseload was before she assigned B. C. Patanjali Elementary School plus 12 additional students (including one homebound and eleven at Mountclair)?

I have worked very hard and have given this job many, many hours of my personal time. My IEP meetings at B. C. Patanjali Elementary School have gone very well. As I continue through this academic year, I must concentrate on the many positive things that have happened at B. C. Patanjali Elementary School.

Fondly,
Katrina Hall
Cc: Shelly Mitchel

On Friday, January 16, 2004, I informed Brenda Craiger of the comprehension scores that my Mountclair students had earned for the second marking period. She suggested that my students could be copying answers, rather than giving me credit for a successful presentation of Reading Mastery. Ludicrous! How could she suggest such a thing? Also, she handed me a copy of her letter dated January 13, 2004. As she handed me this letter, she was literally happy to inform me that this letter would certainly hurt my midyear evaluation. She hated me because I saw through her phoniness, —I saw through her because I was the better person.

On Friday, January 23, 2004, I e-mailed Brenda Craiger to inform her of my conferences with B. C. Patanjali parents. Brenda apparently did not trust me and telephoned Bill to question the validity of this e-mail. I had not informed Bill that I planned to meet with these B. C. Patanjali parents, because it was not required. The fact that Brenda questioned me makes a statement. I feel no matter what I did at Mountclair, I could not win. Every time Brenda observed me, my students were on task, and I was using Reading Mastery, which is what she wanted in her building.

I enjoyed every minute I spent at B. C. Patanjali Elementary School. When Bill Bellkoe walked into my room, I knew he was there to help me become a better teacher. Bill informed me that what I was doing was great, but in addition to what I was doing, I could also do this and that. I loved the post-it notes that he left on my desk after his walkthrough observations! He always began with something positive and then noted possible suggestions! I love reading the post-it notes after he has left my classroom! He made positive suggestions that helped me put together a more productive program for my B. C. Patanjali Elementary School children. My only frustration with B. C. Patanjali was that I was not given sufficient time to instruct.

In addition to having a principal who was helping me to become a better teacher, I had a positive support group from the other teachers at B. C. Patanjali Elementary. I had teachers who complimented my work with their students, and teachers who worked with me.

On Wednesday, February 11, 2004, Brenda Craiger observed me. She always observed me during Reading Group B because this group contained Bobby Brand, a student who was consistently a behavior problem. Bobby was not a behavior problem for me only; he was sent to the principal's office frequently by other teachers as well. Also, Group B was my largest group of students. Brenda Craiger came behind the divider at 2:00 for the beginning of the observation. Bill Bellkoe had helped me prepare for this observation. Brenda Craiger observed the children walking back behind the divider and began asking the students, "Where is Bobby?" When the children began to tell her that Bobby was absent, I noticed the frustration—that look on her face. She was really disappointed because she wanted me to have behavioral problems during my observation! She and I were both well aware of the fact that with Bobby's absence, I would have perfect classroom control during my observation. She was irritated because things went well—the lesson and materials were well organized, the students participated, and she really could not find anything wrong with my instruction. She observed me from 2:00–2:45 PM. At this time I reminded her that I must leave to go to our Special Education Monthly Department Meeting at the District Office. Brenda Craiger replied, "Oh! Well, I didn't know that—I was going to observe you in your 2:45–3:35 Reading Group too. But if you have your meeting, than you must go." I honestly thought that Brenda Craiger was aware of our special education department meeting and that she had planned to observe only one reading group. I don't think any of my observations have ever lasted more than fifty minutes. I asked her if she wanted me to miss the special education department meeting and quickly gather the students of Reading Group C. She informed me that I must go to my department meeting. When I returned to B. C. Patanjali Elementary School, I talked with Bill Bellkoe about this situation. Bill replied, "Well, if she gets snippy with you, just remind her that principals also are included in that e-mail which informs everyone of the scheduled time for the monthly special education department meeting." I told Bill

Bellkoe that I was happy that he informed me of this because Brenda Craiger made me feel as though I had done something wrong. Later, I lamented to Bill Bellkoe the outcome of my observation from Brenda Craiger, informing him that she had given me a marginal score and that *only* my personal hygiene did not need improvement! Bill informed me, "Well, that must have hurt her!"

On April 1, 2004, Shelly Mitchel, the Acting Director of Special Services, observed me. Shelly Mitchel telephoned me at home that evening, and this telephone call meant a lot to me. She complimented me and informed me that it reminded her of a Special Education classroom that she had ran several years earlier in her teaching career. I jokingly asked Shelly Mitchel, "Do I need to improve upon everything except my hygiene?"

Shelly Mitchel replied, "No, certainly not. There is nothing wrong with your instruction; it is you connection with ..." She almost said Brenda Craiger's name, however she finished her sentence with, "other people." Before she had left the building that day, Shelly Mitchel continued to compare the details of my classroom at B. C. Patanjali elementary school to her Special Education classroom, which she had ran, earlier in her teaching career. Shelly Mitchel informed me, "You are working very hard; you go home and you rest!" Unfortunately, there was no rest at home—only household chore after household chore!

I was happy to hear this compliment from Shelly Mitchel. I returned to B. C. Patanjali Elementary School the following morning (4/02/04) and spoke to Bill Bellkoe. I informed him, "Sally called me at home last night! She liked what she saw here (referring to my Special Education classroom at B. C. Patanjali) yesterday when she observed me."

Bill Bellkoe replied, "Yes, I know. She spoke to me before she left the building. Maybe more people are beginning to see what I see."

I was confident after these conversations with Shelly Mitchel and Bill Bellkoe that I would receive a satisfactory evaluation. However, when Sally sent the evaluation form to me (through intra-office mail), she had checked marginal. I was distraught and felt that she had been instructed to check "marginal" by Dr. Marcel Nulldick. Therefore I feel that Shelly Mitchel has violated code #235.11: Professional Relationships. I feel that Shelly Mitchel has knowingly and intentionally distorted my observation/evaluation of April 04, 2004. Shelly Mitchel completed a Clinical Observation Form; however, there was no pre-observation conference because this was a drop-in observation.

I was aware of the fact that I was going to be dismissed in June of 2004 from the Souless Area School District. Therefore I needed to supply future school districts with satisfactory evaluations. I had received a satisfactory evaluation from Bill Bellkoe earlier in the year, however I was aware of the fact that school districts requested spring semester evaluations or the most recent evaluations.

Certainly, an evaluation of marginal or unsatisfactory has impeded my opportunity to gain employment in another local school district. During the month of August 2004, I interviewed with four public school districts, one Christian school, and the local intermediate unit. Each learning institution requested *only* my most recent observation/evaluation sheets. Upon this request, I only supplied Bill Bellkoe's satisfactory evaluation of October 2003. I did not send prospective schools an evaluation that stated my instructional performance as marginal. As a result of this, I was not hired during the 2004–05 academic year.

I feel that Shelly Mitchel has violated code #237.9: Crimes involving moral turpitude. On May 18, 2004, Ms. Shelly Mitchel was intentionally dishonest with me. Shelly Mitchel informed me that my teaching position for the 2004–2005 academic year would consist of B. C. Patanjali, Mike Bergwise, and Mountclair Elementary. I knew Shelly Mitchel was making a dishonest statement because seven of my eleven Mountclair children were fifth grade students who would attend middle school during the 2004–2005 academic year. I was also aware that it was not school policy to put a homebound student in the middle of my day. Also, I had checked with Mrs. Bertha Both, who informed me that her Mountclair caseload for the 2004–2005 year would be approximately twelve students. I felt that Shelly Mitchel was dishonest because she was instructed to do so by Dr. Marcel Nulldick.

Shelly Mitchel is aware of the fact that during the month of August, 2004, surrounding school districts made telephone calls to the Souless Area School District central office, requesting Dr. Marcel Nulldick as a reference. Even though I had not listed Dr. Marcel Nulldick as a reference, other school districts wanted to speak to him.

I have reasons to believe that Shelly Mitchel spoke to a group of Souless Area School District administrators, informing them of my positive qualities as teacher. In May 2004, Shelly Mitchel examined my IEP writing. I e-mailed Shelly Mitchel each of my eight B. C. Patanjali IEPs. I am certain these IEPs were considered well-written documents. I feel the ITAP team was looking for things to hold against me to use for my dismissal. When Shelly Mitchel found that my IEPs were nearly perfect, they could not be used against me as reasons for my dismissal.

I feel that Shelly Mitchel thought highly of my professional performance but was instructed to never discuss my negative situation at Mountclair. I also feel that Shelly Mitchel was instructed by Marcel Nulldick to have little or no contact with me.

I feel that Shelly Mitchel violated code #237.9: Crimes involving moral turpitude. The PDE (Pennsylvania Department of Education) definition includes the following: "(1) That element of personal misconduct in the private and social duties which a person owes to his fellow human beings or to society in general, which characterizes the act done as an act of baseness, vileness, or depravity, and contrary to the accepted and customary rule of right and duty between two human beings. (2) Conduct done knowingly contrary to justice, honesty or good morals. (3) Intentional, knowing or reckless conduct causing bodily injury to another or intentional, knowing or reckless conduct which, by physical menace, puts another in fear of imminent serious bodily injury."

Shelly Mitchel was aware of the fact that Tim Bella's IEP was used against me as part of my 6/02/04 dismissal. Shelly Mitchel was part of the IEP team that witnessed Mrs. Bella sign the NOREP to dismiss Tim Bella from Special Education because, based on the newly administered data, he no longer required special education services. The school psychologist had administered the diagnostic achievement tests and had informed the IEP Team that Tim was intelligent enough to make meaningful progress in the regular education curriculum with no further special education services required. Shelly Mitchel was a witness to the meeting scheduled by the school psychologist of April 2004, in which he informed seven Souless Area School District employees that Tim Bella had tested out of Special Education.

I prepared a "Modified IEP" signed by Mrs. Bella on April 27, 2004. This modified IEP was my way of keeping Tim Bella under my wing until the following school year. Diane Ridgedan helped me complete this modified IEP because I had never completed one prior to Tim Bella's meeting of April 2004. This Modified IEP was held against me, even though I was doing what was best for my special education student. Lisa Vans was his classroom teacher and she was the only weak link. I told Diane Ridgedan that Tim Bella needed to stay with me. Diane Ridgedan instructed me prepare the modified IEP as a method to keep Tim in my classroom, as opposed to Lisa Van's classroom. The staff at B. C. Patanjali

Elementary School was a group of nearly perfect, somewhat seasoned female teachers. The only weak link was Lisa Vans—unfortunately this was Tim's teacher, and she did not treat him with respect. Tim needed to be with me and Diane Ridgedan was well aware of this!

I feel Shelly Mitchel also violated code #237.8: Negligence. According to the PDE (Pennsylvania Department of Education) definition "Negligence is continuing or persistent action or omission in violation of a duty. A Duty may be established by law, by promulgated school rules, policies or procedures, by express direction from superiors or by duties of professional responsibility, including duties prescribed by Chapter 235 (relating to Code of Professional Practice and Conduct for Educators)." It was her duty to acknowledge the fact that the school psychologist scheduled a meeting to inform several Souless Area School District employees that Tim Bella had tested out of special education. Instead, Shelly Mitchel allowed this modified IEP to be used against me.

Bertha Both assigned eleven of her special education students to me. Mrs. Bertha Both gave me the students with behavioral problems and the curriculum (scripted reading) that she found least desirable; Diane Ridgedan will attest to that. Bertha Both assigned herself ample planning time at my expense. I feel I have been taken advantage of by Bertha Both, and that she has violated Code #235.4: Practices. Bertha Both failed to "exhibit consistent and equitable treatment of students, (and) fellow educators." She was deceitful with her schedule. Diane Ridgedan informed Bertha Both not to give me eleven Mountclair children however Bertha Both did not listen. Bertha Both gave herself thirty-five minutes per day to "Assist Katrina with Reading Mastery." Bertha Both *never* assisted me with anything; she used that time for an additional planning time, or socializing time, or eating time, or relaxing time, or free time. The fact that Brenda Craiger condoned this made the rage that I experienced unbearable! I did not even have a bathroom break—I was taken advantage of, sabotaged, and undermined by Bertha Both and Brenda Craiger! I feel Bertha Both was rude and unethical. Bertha Both erected a room divider inside her classroom, and behind this room divider she placed a table with six chairs. I have included a diagram of Bertha Both 's classroom because I feel it is a significant factor in my account of this academic year.

I feel that Bertha Both has violated code #237.9: Crimes involving moral turpitude. In September 2003, Bertha Both spoke negatively to me about Mindy Rissmiller, a student. I had already grown to enjoy and develop a rapport with Mindy Rissmiller. I informed Bertha Both, "Please do not say anything negative about Mindy Rissmiller in front of me, because I love that child." Mindy Rissmiller lived in a car during the 2002–2003 school year when she was Bertha Both 's student. Mindy Rissmiller lived in a trailer with no windows and minimal heat during the 2003–2004 school year when she was my student. Many special education textbooks inform us of the low-income families who are frequently parents of special education children. I was shocked when Bertha Both, a special education teacher of seventeen years, spoke negatively about Mindy Rissmiller.

I feel that Bertha Both has violated code # 237.3: Immorality. Bertha Both frequently whispered negative comments about my teaching performance to her aide, Debbie. Debbie sat where I could see her from behind the divider. I could hear Bertha Both whispering, although I could not see Bertha Both, and then I could see Debbie laughing at me. Therefore Bertha Both "set a bad example to the youth" who were my students. My students noticed the behavior of Bertha Both and made comments to me. Every day I left Mountclair Elementary so upset I could barely drive. It was my first year, and I had had no experience teaching from a scripted reading program. It took a few weeks for me to become familiar with the materials and this type of instruction.

I feel Bertha Both has violated code #235.4: Practices. Bertha Both failed to "exhibit acceptable and professional language and communication skills." Bertha Both 's "verbal and written communications with … staff" did not reflect sensitivity to the fundamental human rights of dignity, privacy and respect." I feel that Bertha Both was, on numerous occasions, saying negative things about my performance to Brenda Craiger. I felt uncomfortable because she listened to every word I said to my students. She frequently yelled out remarks; for example, without getting out of her seat, she would reprimand one of my students from behind the divider for an inappropriate behavior. I constantly felt that Bertha Both and Debbie, her aide, were listening to every word I said to those children. Therefore Bertha Both violated code #235.11: Professional Relationships. Bertha Both knowingly and intentionally denied and impeded my right to enjoy my classes at Mountclair Elementary School.

After December 19, 2003, Debbie, Bertha Both 's aide, was given other responsibilities. I was informed that this was because Marcel Nulldick reprimanded Bertha Both for taking advantage of me. I handed Marcel Nulldick a copy of Bertha Both's schedule—a schedule approved by Brenda Craiger, principal of a school of favorites.

Bertha Both frequently ate turkey burger and desserts with whipped cream inside the classroom (while I was teaching) on the other side of the divider. My students frequently complained of the odor of turkey burger as they entered the classroom. The sound of the whipped cream being sprayed onto a dessert was a daily distraction to my students. They giggled and whispered fat jokes. On the other hand, I barely had time to fit in bathroom breaks. Day after day I sat behind the divider while Bertha Both gave herself the afternoon off! The same situation occurred at home and work, domestically and professionally. At school I watched Bertha Both relax, have casual conversations with her friends, and eat lots of food, while I was overwhelmed and inundated with students and teaching materials. At home I was overwhelmed with household chores, while I watched my husband sitting in the recliner holding the remote in his hand. It made the internal rage and anger rise! Had I created this life through negative emotional energy? I had been taken advantage of both professionally and domestically! I wonder what Dr. Wayne Dyer would say about this. He has stated, "The people who get the most respect in the world are those who are the straightest, even though they often take the most abuse." He has also said, "You become what you think about all day long, and those days become your lifetime," and, "You're the creator of your thoughts, which means that in some metaphysical way, you're the creator of your life." Had I created this life in which I was emotionally tortured both professionally and domestically?

I feel that Bertha Both has violated code #237.8: Negligence. According to the PDE (Pennsylvania Department of Education) the definition of negligence is "continuing or persistent action or omission in violation of a duty. A Duty may be established by law, by promulgated school rules, policies or procedures, by express direction from superiors or by duties of professional responsibility, including duties prescribed by Chapter 235 (relating to Code of Professional Practice and Conduct for Educators)."

I was in many instances blamed for Bertha Both 's negligence. For example, Bertha Both allowed Mindy Rissmiller's IEP to expire during the 2002-2003 school year. During fall of the 2003–2004 year, this child moved into the B. C. Patanjali jurisdiction. Mindy Rissmiller came to me with an expired IEP. As I look back on this now I cannot imagine a special education teacher with seventeen years experience allowing an IEP to expire. However, I was blamed for Bertha Both 's negligence. I asked Bertha Both if I could see Mindy Rissmiller's DAB (Diagnostic Achievement Battery) scores from the 2002–2003 academic year so that I could begin to prepare a new IEP. She informed me that she had not bothered to administer this diagnostic test. Once again, she openly admitted that she had been negligent. I asked Bertha if she could instruct me on how to use the DAB (Diagnostic Achievement Battery) test, and she informed me that she had *never* used it. Bertha Both was required to give each special education student one diagnostic test per academic year. Therefore during the 2002--2003 academic year, Bertha Both neglected to fulfill this responsibility. Bertha Both neglected to administer the required diagnostic achievement to Mindy Rissmiller; she also neglected to write an updated IEP, simply allowing the IEP to be out of compliance.

When I confronted Bertha Both, she acted as if she didn't even care, and she gave me some lame asinine excuse. She told me she did not write an IEP for Mindy Rissmiller because the school district from which Mindy had moved out of had failed to send Bertha her existing IEP and other pertinent documents. So why didn't she get on the telephone with the guidance counselor and request those documents? Why didn't she use her seventeen years of teaching experience in the field of special education and create a fresh IEP based on newly administered diagnostic data?

Dr. Lurk blamed me for the IEP of Mindy Rissmiller being out of compliance. I received a memo indicating that I had neglected my responsibilities. I discussed this memo with Bill Bellkoe, who informed me that "this is your first strike against you." In response to Dr. Lurk's memo, I wrote to Dr. James Ryan, the Superintendent, in defense of these accusations. I first explained that Bertha Both had allowed this IEP to expire during the previous academic year and that Mindy Rissmiller had came to me with an expired IEP. Then I went through a list of dates and activities which I needed to complete prior to administering the DAB (Diagnostic Achievement Battery) test to Mindy Rissmiller. I needed first to meet with the school psychologist and gather the appropriate materials. Second, I needed to meet with the student when I was not in the classroom at B. C. Patanjali Elementary School. My instruction time at B.C. Patanjali Elementary School was very limited, and fitting in additional time for testing a student one on one was incredibly difficult for me to do. Dr. Lurk was aware of the steps I needed to complete before the IEP of Mindy Rissmiller could be written. Each step consumed another school day. I should not have been the teacher to receive this memo—it should have been Bertha Both. I was blamed for her laziness, however she was one of Brenda Craiger's favorite teachers, and she therefore got away with everything!

In May 2004 Bertha Both and I were instructed to work together preparing IEP goals for several students for the 2004–2005 academic year. I asked Bertha Both several times to stay after school so that we could prepare these goals together. Bertha Both made excuses regarding working with me on preparing these goals. For example, she informed me she "really did not have time." I asked Bertha Both on three separate occasions to stay after school and work with me. Bertha never helped me; however her schedule allowed her thirty minutes per day for 180 days to help me! How did Bertha Both sleep at night? She refused to work with me, but she instructed me to give all three children the same goals because she planned on placing them in same reading group during the 2004–2005 academic year.I informed her that I did not agree that these three children should be grouped together. I informed Bertha Both several times that these children had very different learning abilities and reading levels. I prepared the reading goals at home with no assistance from Bertha Both. (This was a perfect example of how my entire year went.)

It is ludicrous that I was blamed for the negligence of Bertha Both, who had seventeen years experience as a special education teacher. The fact that I had been blamed for her negligence made the rage inside me rise, and I felt overwhelmed with anger! I was certain that Brenda Craiger directed Bertha Both to make our working together inconvenient for me so that Brenda could report to Marcel Nulldick! I am positive that Brenda Craiger told Marcel Nulldick that I intentionally had not worked with Bertha Both on goal writing! The 2003–2004 academic year was my first year of teaching.

Midyear I spoke with Bertha Both regarding reading levels of the eleven Mountclair children. I did not feel that these children were grouped according to ability—Three of my children had had the same reading book for two consecutive academic years! This was an outrage in itself! If one never administered new words, how would the students progress? They must be exposed to new reading books and new reading materials. That was a disgrace to hear her make such a statement, openly, like she did not even care! I questioned Bertha Both 's basis for grouping these children. Bertha Both informed me, "I look at scheduling more than I do abilities." This was evident in the fact that she gave herself ample planning time at the expense of the students and me.

I feel that Bertha Both violated code #237.7: Cruelty. On May 3, 2004, I asked Bertha Both if she could stay with my reading group while I ran two doors down the hall to purchase a water bottle. She replied "No!" and informed me that she had an IST (Instructional Support Team) meeting to attend—this was an IST meeting, *not* an IEP meeting! I was not surprised, remembering back to an earlier instance (possibly November) when Bertha Both denied me a bathroom break.

On May 19, 2004, a field day was planned for all elementary special education students. The elementary children were to be paired with Souless Area School District senior high students. The events of the day included fair activities and competitive activities such as races. The day also included snacks and facial painting. I was very excited to think how wonderful it would be to have the opportunity to enjoy a different type of day with the children I had grown to love and adore throughout the 2003-2004 school year.

Bertha Both did not want to attend this event. I inquired why, wondering what reason she would have for depriving these special education students of such an enjoyable day. Bertha Both informed me that she simply did not want to deal with those kids! Diane Ridgedan intervened, and both my B. C. Patanjali children and my Mountclair children attended. I was happy when Diane Ridgedan intervened because if Bertha Both had refused to attend, I would have been stuck with teaching scripted reading to the Mountclair students. My eight B. C. Patanjali students would have been forced to miss the event because I would not have been able to take them.

Significantly, it was Bertha Both's duty to instruct these children. My name is not on any of the Mountclair IEPs. The only Special Education teacher listed is Bertha Both. Bertha Both, another special education teacher, assigned my caseload. There were no administrators present when Bertha Both decided that she would have ample planning time, while I would have 100 percent instruction time.

I feel that Bertha Both has violated code #237.9: Crimes involving moral turpitude. She conducted herself in a manner of baseness, contrary to what is honorable and right between two teachers sharing a classroom. I feel that I was taken advantage of and treated unprofessionally and disrespectfully in every way by Bertha Both. One day that is outstanding in my mind is the day that another teacher was sent into Bertha Both's room to observe me. The children noticed this teacher in the room, and her presence was a distraction. This occurred during the month of October 2003. I feel that Brenda Craiger initiated this. If this situation is taken into litigation, I will have this teacher subpoenaed. On this day I was behind the divider with five Mountclair children. On the other side of the divider, Bertha Both was eating, Shannon Mackley was writing vigorously, and Debbie, the aide, was listening to every word of instruction that I said to those children. I could hear the three of them whispering and giggling! This is a perfect example of how my entire year went—there were four adults in that room, and I was the only person responsible for instruction.

I feel that Bertha Both violated code #235.4: Practices. On January 8, 2004, a Mountclair student felt that he did not need to obey me because I was "different" and was not "permanent." Therefore, confidential information about my credentials had been spoken about in front of students.

I feel that Bertha Both violated code #237.5: Intemperance. According to the PDE (Pennsylvania Department of Education, Intemperance is defined as "a loss of self-control or self restraint, which may result from excessive conduct." On January 30, 2004, Bertha Both had friends in her classroom. (She assigned no students to herself while I had 100 percent instruction time at Mountclair.) Their talking was extremely loud, and the children were distracted. The children mentioned (to me) how loud Bertha Both and her friends were talking.

On one occasion, a student asked me, "Why are so many of us stuck behind this divider, and Mrs. Both has all that room and no students?" Another incident that is outstanding in my mind is the day when Bertha Both 's substitute informed me, "I have nothing to do, and you have so many children back there. Is there anything that I can do to help you?"

I felt sadness for Bertha Both because she was obese and immature. She lacked emotional maturity and emotional intelligence. She had no children, only dogs. I was going home to a family who loved me, and she was going home to dogs. She had no children—perhaps that is why she was emotionally immature. There is no better reason for growth and change than to be a better role model to one's biological children. When I thought about the life of Bertha Both, I felt sympathy because she did not gain joy from helping others.

If the situation had been reversed, I would *not* have taken advantage of a new special education teacher—I would have enjoyed helping that person. I would have enjoyed sharing some of the wonderful things that I had learned in my years in the classroom. I always feel joy when I help other people with things. My sympathy for her was due to the fact that she would never experience the joy of loving biological children; she would never enjoy watching them grown and mature; she would not be motivated to experience more personal growth so that she can be a better role model to her children; she would continue to miss out on the joy that one experiences when helping another person; she would never experience the energetic, healthy lifestyle of a slender person. She will never understand the elation of serotonin. I am glad I am I am the opposite of Bertha Both.

The endless list of unfair, twisted, sabotaging, undermined things that happened to me during the 2003–2004 academic year makes me crazy! The intense internal anger and rage that I feel when I think about them makes me want to explode. Why were these people so hurtful toward me? How could they behave in this unethical manner and show no remorse?

"No, Not Today!"

On Thursday, January 26, 2003, Brenda Craiger placed a note in every teacher mailbox *except mine* informing the faculty that Dr. James Ryan, the superintendent, would be in the building. Brenda Craiger knew exactly when my reading groups changed classes. She was quite aware that during the last three minutes of my scheduled reading groups, my students would be instructed to get out of their seats and put away their materials. She attempted to bring the superintendent in Bertha Both's classroom to perform a walkthrough observation while my students were putting away their materials so that I could dismiss them. She intentionally timed it this way. Did such conniving and deceitful behavior bring her joy?

I was behind the divider with five low-level reading students when I heard Dr. James Ryan's voice! Brenda Craiger was leading the way behind the divider, and I heard Dr. Ryan's voice. When he saw the divider, he asked Brenda Craiger, "Is this …?" Then he whispered, "Katrina?"

Brenda replied, "Yes!"

Dr. James Ryan announced, "No, not today!" They stood in the door way of Bertha Both's classroom and had a conversation. I could hear Brenda Craiger's phony voice because it contained a tone of annoyance toward Dr. James Ryan!

She informed him, "But the children are out of their seats!" That conniving principal timed the superintendent's walk through so that he could see my students putting away their materials—which gave her the opportunity to make such a statement! Brenda Criager exhibited unethical behavior throughout the academic year. I have never met anyone as intentionally hurtful; how does she sleep at night, and when does she have time to plan such vindictiveness? Does she not have a school to run? I knew exactly how she had timed things, and I knew exactly why she took that letter out of my mailbox. I saw through every vindictive and phony action of Brenda Craiger! When I heard them talking in the doorway, I wanted to stand up and defend myself—I wanted Dr. James Ryan, Superintendent, to know that Brenda Craiger timed it this way just to make me look bad. If these two administrators had walked in fifteen minutes earlier, they would have observed a well-planned Reading Mastery lesson, with a reading group well under control and all students fully engaged in their work.

On Friday, January 29, 2004, Bertha Both and her friends were talking so loudly that they were distracting my students! The students complained that they could not hear me, and I could hardly continue my instruction over the loud socialization on the other side of the divider! This was such a distraction—and how unprofessional of her. It wasn't bad enough that my students and I always had to smell her turkey burger which she consumed—now I had to teach over the distractions of loud socialization! Where were Dr. James Ryan, Superintendent, and the tyrant Brenda Craiger that day? The day before at this exact time, they were standing in the doorway (of Bertha Both's domain) having a conversation about my students putting away their reading materials. I know Bertha was tipped off—Brenda had told her stay out of her room when Dr. James Ryan was in the building on Thursday, 1/29/2004. After all, how would it look to the superintendent to have Bertha Both sitting, dawdling, socializing, and eating, while Katrina Hall was instructing back-to-back groups of low-level students? Perhaps the superintendent would realize that Brenda was running a school of favorites, and perhaps Brenda Craiger and Bertha Both would have been fired in June 2004 instead of me!

Whenever I entered the Mountclair Elementary School building, I did so through the backdoor because I knew I must use my swipe card to enter. After all, this was similar to a movie with bad cops, and I felt I could trust no one—especially in Brenda Craiger's building! One day Bertha Both put a note on my table behind the divider telling me that I would have no students that day. Therefore I ran errands within the building, made copies, looked over future reading lessons, and made additional trips to the copier preparing lesson plans for the following week. The next thing I knew, Brenda Craiger's secretary had been instructed to find me because the students of Group B Reading Class were alone, waiting behind the divider—for me! After school, I asked Bertha Both why she put such a note on my table. She stated a stupid remark of a lie, telling me that she thought the students would not see me that day, but their regular classroom activity must not have lasted as long as anticipated. What a crock! She sabotaged me!

Similarly, I was very ill one day when I left Mountclair Elementary School and knew I would be too sick to work the next day. Therefore I wrote out lesson plans for my substitute for the next day. I was very careful to write the word SUBSTITUTE in large, black capital letters on the front of a blue folder containing detailed lesson plans, and I placed this blue folder on my table behind the divider. When the substitute arrived the next day, the folder was gone. The substitute told Bertha Both that he could not find any lesson plans. Bertha immediately contacted Brenda Craiger. When I returned I had a note in my Mountclair faculty mailbox—which was really Bertha's mailbox—informing me to promptly meet with Brenda Craiger at 3:20 PM. When I originally read the note, I had no idea that my substitute had never received my lesson plans! However, I began to prepare myself for the upcoming 3:20 PM tirade and harangue!

After teaching my three back-to-back reading groups, I walked down the dreaded hall to Brenda Craiger's office. She was outraged, and she let me have it. "In seventeen years, I have never seen anything like this!" I asked Brenda Craiger what she was talking about. She informed me that my substitute had not been provided with lesson plans. I was shocked! I told her that I had written out detailed lesson plans, had placed them in a labeled blue folder, containing the word SUBSTITUE in large black letters, and had placed the folder on my table behind the divider in Bertha's room. She replied, "Okay, if you did them, then I want you to go back to Bertha's room and get them." I walked back to Bertha's room, distraught as usual, which was consistently the result of talking with Brenda Craiger. Fortunately, Bertha was still in her classroom, and I questioned her. She said, "Oh, I'm sorry—I had some students working at the table back there, and I put your blue folder on the shelf." I looked around my area behind the divider and could not see them so I asked her "Where?" She walked back behind the divider and showed me—she had stuck my lesson plans on the top bookshelf—between books! No wonder the substitute *never* found it! I asked her why she didn't return the folder to my table when the students were finished their work. She replied, "I must have forgotten." But this teacher who hid my lesson plans from the substitute didn't forget to tell Brenda Craiger on me! I took the blue folder back to the tyrant's (Brenda Craiger's) office and handed it to her. She did *not* look at the assignments and lesson plans inside—she didn't even open the folder—and she just said, "So this is what you did? This is inadequate. I am going to tell Dr. Marcel Nulldick that you left inadequate substitute plans!" She didn't even look at them! The rage and anger made me crazy. Why was Brenda Craiger so evil? Why was Bertha Both so cruel and dishonest? Why? What lesson did God want me to learn from this horrible and heinous experience?

One day the Reading Specialist at Mountclair, Katrina Elkind, put a note on my desk asking me to see her before I left the building. My Group A reading students were attending an assembly, and therefore I went immediately to Katrina Elkind's classroom to talk with her. I asked her what she wanted, and she replied, "We share many of the same students, and I just wanted to see how they were doing." I informed her that would run back to Bertha Both's classroom and get my grade book. After being in close proximity with Katrina Elkind, I instinctively knew that Brenda Craiger had directed Katrina to write that note. Brenda Craiger was always looking for ways to make me look bad—she wanted to find negative behaviors so that she could document things against me. When there was nothing negative to document—because I had consistently performed my teaching position duties and fulfilled all of my professional responsibilities—she was then forced to falsify information—which was a real talent of hers.

I had developed a rapport with the School Nurse. Because it was a small district, the school nurse worked in two buildings, B. C. Patanjali Elementary and Mountclair Elementary. I was first introduced to the School Nurse the day of my car accident. Since then, she and I had shared many friendly conversations. One day at B. C. Patanjali, I said hello to her, and she practically replied, "I just wanted you to know that I think Brenda Craiger is a very fair administrator." Based on our close proximity, I instinctively knew that Dr. Marcel Nulldick had instructed her to say that! It was an odd conversation, atypical of our usual, friendly chats—she didn't even segue into the statement--she just blurted it out! Amazing how much influence this person had over people who wanted to keep their jobs. If he had told people to murder someone, they probably would have listened to him just to remain employed at this backwoods school district!

Routinely during my Group B reading class, Bertha Both took three children on her caseload into Shannon Mackley's classroom for math instruction. Bertha Both had mentioned to me that it was easier this way because "Why not let Shannon be responsible for the instruction and the lesson plans and the grading?" It was so much less work for Bertha to just let Shannon do everything! Bertha Both had given herself the easiest schedule ever, and always at the expense of others doing more work—actually doing her share of the work load. Bertha Both did this to me, to Gracie Ling, and to Shannon Mackley. One day, as my reading students were entering Bertha's classroom and walking behind the divider, I noticed that Bertha also had three children seated in her very spacious classroom. I thought how odd this was—she was actually instructing. I was suspicious but did not ask her why she was teaching on that specific day. I continued on with my reading group instruction. Suddenly, Brenda Craiger and Dr. Marcel Nulldick walked through Bertha Both's door! They were performing a walkthrough observation! I felt that my moment of empowerment was here! Two administrators who had already formulated a negative opinion of me were standing side by side in Brenda's domain and on Bertha's turf!

It was odd because Marcel had a nervous smile on his face, and he frequently looked nervous when he was speaking. After all, I was the one being observed—not him. At one of our monthly special education meetings, his voice quivered—he sounded like he was going to have a nervous breakdown—so how would he endure the public speaking responsibilities of an assistant superintendent? I felt sorry for him because it had only taken me about two weeks to overcome my fear of public speaking. (Bill actually brought this to my attention one day and said to me in a friendly tone, "But you are over that now!") Brenda hated the fact that I remained calm while I was instructing! Brenda always had a phony smile on her face when she was in front of Marcel and in my presence. I knew it was phony and I wondered if Marcel ever saw through Brenda's phony behaviors. When Brenda was alone with me, she consistently treated me in an unprofessional and rude manner. Walk-through observations are supposed to be unannounced to the teacher under observation. I instinctively and instantly knew that Brenda Craiger had told Bertha Both not to take those children into Shannon Mackley's room that day. Brenda Craiger was nothing but an evil conniver, and she Brenda Craiger, principal of a school of favorites, tipped off Bertha Both! Lazy Bertha Both knew that Dr. Marcel Nulldick was scheduled to observe me and her simultaneously. Brenda Craiger and Marcel Nulldick stood there together, behind the aide's desk, so that they could see both me and Bertha. My students were well behaved, my reading lesson was going well, and my students were engaged in active instruction the entire time Brenda and

Marcel were standing in Bertha's classroom. I am certain that Marcel Nulldick never knew that Brenda Craiger tipped off Bertha Both.

Bertha Both was supposed to share all the Reading Mastery materials with me. Actually, there was no sharing—she was not using them because she had given all the work to me. She had delegated to me the least desirable form of instruction—scripted reading. One day Brenda Craiger asked me to locate the placement test for the Reading Mastery (scripted reading) program. I immediately walked back to Bertha's classroom and told her that Brenda wanted to see the placement tests. All the materials were locked in a closet in Bertha Both's classroom. Bertha told me that no placement tests existed for that specific Reading Mastery program. She didn't even bother to unlock her closet and look for them. She had seventeen years experience and should have been familiar with such materials. I walked back to Brenda's office and informed her that they did not exist. Surprise! Surprise! Bertha had lied to me. After I left the building, Brenda walked to Bertha's classroom, and Bertha gave Brenda the requested Reading Mastery placement tests.

When I returned to Mountclair the next day, there was a familiar note in the faculty mail box that instructed me to see Brenda at 3:20 PM. From 1:00 to 3:20 PM I dreaded the usual tirade and harangue! I dreaded it and had to hide my anger while I was teaching my three back-to-back scripted reading groups. Finally, between groups of students entering and leaving Bertha's classroom, I managed to have a short conversation with Bertha. I asked her why she told me they didn't exist. She told me that she really thought she didn't have them. Of course, she was not familiar with the reading materials because she had always found someone else to do her dirty work. (During the previous academic year, she had used Gracie Ling; during the 2003–2004 academic year, she used me—all condoned by Brenda Craiger.) Scripted reading is not enjoyable to teach—you could sit a child in front of a computer program and produce similar results. After she had informed me that they did not exist I left the building; then Brenda entered Bertha's room requesting the nonexistent placement tests. Bertha immediately unlocked the closet and handed Brenda the appropriate Reading Mastery placement tests!

When I entered Brenda's office, I could feel the negativity and depleting energy—the close proximity always made me crazy. It was especially intense when Brenda and I were alone together in her office. It was as if the walls were telling me that I was not the only teacher Brenda had abused and tortured! There had been many others tortured by the tyrant through the years, and their negative energy, in the form of anger and rage, still existed inside Brenda's office. Brenda asked me why I had not looked for them. I explained to her that Bertha had told me they did not exist; therefore I did not bother to look for something that did not exist. Should I have told Bertha that I did not believe her and ask her to get the closet key for me? I didn't know Bertha was being dishonest with me just to create more professional turbulence in my life.

Bill Bellkoe had requested that I prepare lesson plans based on the anticipatory set, which I enjoyed doing. Based on this idea, students are given some type of reward at the end of a lesson. One reward idea was to allow the children to draw a picture for five minutes or less, after having completed a lesson or required academic task. The short-reward system worked well because it motivated students to stay focused so that the reward could be earned. One day at Mountclair I had finished an entire reading lesson with the Group A reading group. Their reward was to have five minutes at the end of the lesson to draw a picture. The students worked well and completed all academic activities, and then they each received one sheet of construction paper and a few crayons. They enjoyed this five-minute reward and had earned it! They were dismissed from my reading class and returned to their regular education classroom. They were excited about their pictures and showed their regular education classroom teacher, Miss Laura Knoll. Miss Laura Knoll collected the pictures from the students and went directly to Brenda's office and told Brenda that I had allowed the children to draw pictures. Brenda contacted Dr. Lurk and made several negative accusations about these pictures.

The next morning when I arrived at B. C. Patanjali Elementary School, I received a telephone call from Dr. Lurk, the Supervisor of Special Education. She asked me why I had allowed the children to draw pictures. I informed her that this was a five-minute reward and that the children had finished their reading lesson for the day. I also reminded her that according to the teaching procedures manual, which I had thoroughly gone through, the students were supposed to complete one lesson per day. I had also discussed the pace of presentation of Reading Mastery with several other professionals who had a background in reading. Based on the way the program was set up, one lesson per day was the proper presentation. Dr. Lurk was very kind to me because I was hysterical on the telephone with her that morning. My friend, a janitor, came by to comfort me. That afternoon, certainly, I saw the infamously dreaded note from Brenda inside the faculty mailbox. She directed me to meet in her office at 3:20 PM. I was forced to instruct students all afternoon with the dread of our meeting. I entered Brenda Craiger's office and received her look of disgust and hate, and I felt everything negative that could exist between two people. She handed me the children's pictures, and I informed her that I had done this as a reward, that this reward system was based on the strategies set forth by the anticipatory set procedure for preparing lesson plans, that the reading lesson had been completed, that this reward consumed less than five minutes of my instruction time, and that I had already spoken to Dr. Lurk. Brenda Craiger of course questioned me—it didn't matter what I had to say, it didn't matter how intensely I tried to explain myself. Brenda went off on her usual tirade and harangue! She rudely handed me the pictures! Brenda always made me feel powerless and incompetent; she made me feel so bad inside. Once again I left her office and Mountclair Elementary School in a state of hysteria! Miss Laura Knoll would not make eye contact with me during the days following this event. She must have experienced some remorse for her devious actions against me. She had done something vindictive to a person she did not know personally or professionally. I believe in karma. Certainly, Miss Laura Knoll was one of Brenda's favorites. I also felt sorry for her because she had such a fear of public speaking—sometimes when we would meet to discuss the progress of our reading students, she sounded as nervous as Dr. Marcel Nulldick. How many years do these people have to do this job before they get over their fear of public speaking? I am strong and got over my fear of public speaking in about two weeks!

My Mentor

My mentor, Kara Keep, worked in another elementary building in the Souless Area School District. This was unfortunate for me because I had little contact with her. For the most part it was not her fault because she was busy—but it was inconvenient for us to work together. I really had no contact with her until late October 2003. At this point I felt that Bill Bellkoe directed her to contact me. I received a card through interoffice mail that told me to hang in there.

I had made arrangements to meet with Kara Keep before school one morning. This meeting was scheduled for 7:15 AM in the elementary building where Kara Keep worked, before Kara and I began our teaching day. I got out of bed an hour earlier than usual and drove an extra twenty minutes to Kara's building. She did not arrive until it was ten minutes before homeroom! She apologized profusely, explaining that she had forgotten. Not only had she forgotten, but she had arrived to her building much later than usual because she had run errands before she came to school. There were many instances in which I needed a quick special education question answered so that I could complete my work and remain in compliance. Because I was the only special education teacher in B. C. Patanjali Elementary School, I had no support. There is a reason why public school districts provide mentors to newly hired teachers. It was really to my disadvantage that my mentor was twenty minutes away from me in a different building.

Kara Keep had previously worked at B. C. Patanjali Elementary School as a special education teacher. For a few years Dr. Lurk allowed Karen to stay in B. C. Patanjali all day, even though she only had a small number of special education students on her caseload. However, the two years previous to my employment, Dr. Lurk scheduled her in the senior high building, giving her a variety of responsibilities, but no caseload. For this reason, Kara Keep left B. C. Patanjali Elementary School, and accepted a position in another elementary building within the same district, simply because she wanted to stay in the same building all day.

One day I asked Karen Keep how many students she had on her caseload at B. C. Patanjali Elementary School. She hesitated and then replied, "I don't remember." I instinctively knew that Dr. Marcel Nulldick had told her to say this. I can always tell when people are being dishonest with me—I guess you could say that it is a gift. I remember having this same conversation with her earlier in the academic year, and I recall Kara telling me that her B. C. Patanjali Elementary caseload was from three to five students per year!!

Shredded Lesson Plans

One day in December 2003, Brenda Craiger called me into her office. She asked me why I had not placed my weekly lesson plans in Bertha Both's lesson plan folder. I informed her that I was certain I had done so. Located next to the teacher lesson plan file, there was a shredding machine. I knew exactly what had happened to my lesson plans that week! Bertha Both had taken my lesson plans out of the folder and shredded them when no one was looking. I told Diane Ridgedan about this, and she replied, "But Bertha Both would not do that!" Diane Ridgedan was so nice to me, and she was certainly a person of integrity—Diane would not do that—but Bertha Both would. It is hard to believe what others can do, what heinous acts people are capable of performing is inconceivable to good people like Diane Ridgedan.

I was enduring professional adversity! I was living a professional dichotomy! Every day for 180 days, I had this wonderful position at a perfect school—things were going well, my students were making academic progress, and I had many friends in the building at B. C. Patanjali Elementary School. The principal thought highly of me—although in the very beginning of the year, I had to work extra hard to gain his professional respect. I loved the students, and I loved preparing their weekly lesson plans. Then I would leave to go to my homebound student and then to Mountclair. I hated it! Brenda Craiger was out to get me fired, and she did not let up. By the time I left B. C. Patanjali, my head was already spinning from the work load—it was overwhelming! Then I had to deal with my homebound student, who was severely disabled. His mother was in denial regarding the reality of her son's disability. Every day I cried as I was driving toward Mountclair Elementary School, never knowing what evil and adversity awaited me during my afternoon reading lessons. I wanted to drive away from Mountclair—not toward it. One cold winter day, I was leaving my homebound student's residence, and the roads were filled with snow. My little 1988 Toyota Celica was not the best in snow; I loved this car and wished that new tires were not so expensive. I just sat there for a few minutes in the private driveway. I wanted so much to drive home! But I did not go home—I went to Mountclair to deal with the usual professional adversity.

One Weak Link

Lisa Vans was B. C. Patanjali Elementary School's only weak link. The faculty members were seasoned teachers who were extremely dedicated to the profession. My B. C. Patanjali caseload numbers peaked at eight, and four of these learning-disabled students were in Lisa Vans's regular education fourth grade classroom. From the very beginning of school in August 2003, Lisa had made it very clear to me that she did not want these special education students in her classroom. I informed Shannon Mackley of this, during a casual conversation, and she replied, "Of course she doesn't want them, because they are extra work." From my room, classroom #112, I could see through the entrance into Lisa's classroom. One day I noticed that she embarrassed Gary Reel in front of the entire class. I heard her raise her voice to Gary, and I watched his face turn bright red! One day, when it was time for the learning-disabled students to leave my room, she sent them back to me. Tim Bella led the group back into my room and said, "She told us we weren't allowed to come in." One day she made little Sally cry in front of the class, just out of pure frustration. I loved my B. C. Patanjali children, and I therefore kept them with me long past the required time. According to special education regulations and the IEP of each child, I was keeping them several more hours per week than I was legally supposed to. As the school year progressed, the emotional attachment that I had for each child grew simultaneously; as did the hours they spent with me in my classroom #112.

Many days my homebound student was too ill for instruction; his mother would telephone Bonnie, B. C. Patanjali Elementary School's secretary, and inform me not to come to the home today. I tried so hard to have sympathy in my voice, but deep inside I was so happy when she canceled on me! When Mrs. Bergwise canceled on me, it gave me more time at B. C. Patanjali Elementary School! I loved my job at B. C. Patanjali Elementary School, and I wanted to spend more time there, teaching my learning disabled students academic concepts and reading and math skills. I loved the school, I loved the principal, I had a rapport with the teachers, and the other professionals in B. C. Patanjali respected me and told me what a good job I was doing. On days when Mrs. Bergwise canceled, I would keep my B. C. Patanjali children until their lunch break at 11:45. They would come to me as soon as they got off the school bus in the morning, check in with Lisa for attendance, and come directly to my room.

There were days when Lisa would not bother to take them to their elementary specials such as art class or library period. As the year went on the children wanted to stay with me more and more because they were well aware who wanted to be with them. Children instinctively know things like that—they pick up emotional connections and positive vibes more easily than do adults; their sensitivities and natural instincts are stronger than most adults. There were some days when the children stayed with me from 8:50 AM to almost 1:00 PM, when I needed to leave for Mountclair Elementary School. Bill Bellkoe and Diane Ridgedan knew the situation—that Lisa Vans really did not want these children in her regular education classroom, and that she did not work well with slow learners. She just was not patient enough, she was not kind enough, and she did not want to bother with the extra work. Sometimes when Mrs. Bergwise canceled on me, the children would miss recess and spend the time in my classroom.

I never really found out how Bill Bellkoe and Marcel Nulldick got wind of this, but somehow they became aware that Lisa's special education students were in my classroom much longer than they were in her classroom. According to state special education regulations, this violated FAPE—their right to a Free and Appropriate Education in the Least Restricted Environment (LRE). Bill Bellkoe called me into his office and informed me that children must have limited amounts of time in my room. He also informed me that Marcel Nulldick had stated, "Katrina is not Lisa's babysitter!" It was Spring (Wednesday, March 31, 2004) when Bill and Marcel gave Lisa and I strict directives regarding specific times slots for each of us. I had been given the directive to schedule these children for reading and math lessons with me—otherwise they should *not* be in my room and should remain in Lisa's classroom. Therefore during most of the school year, I had spent a great deal more time with these children than did Lisa. Thank God! I was saddened because I wanted to work with these children all day long. I was so happy because I knew I was the teacher who taught Tim Bella how to do long division. I worked with him and stayed patient, until one day I saw the light go on and he got it! Tim and I were so excited; we shared our academic successes with the other children in my classroom. The next day we celebrated and I brought in a treat—after all, everyone needed a little candy every once in a while! The children continually verbalized how much they wanted to be with me and not with Mrs. Vans. Children are always honest! One day Gary said, "I want to stay here with you because you are nice to us, and she is mean!" The other children joined in and pleaded with me to let them stay longer like they used to do. However, after receiving the following document from Bill Bellkoe, I was well aware of the fact that I must follow his directive.

To: Teachers of Special Education Students
From: Bill Bellkoe
Subject: Resource Room Placement
Date: 3/31/2004

> *It has come to my attention that some special education students are out of their regular classrooms more than the allowed time.*
>
> *All of our special education students have a requirement for "less than 21 percent outside of the regular classroom." These students may not be pulled out more than seventy-five minutes per day.*
>
> *Katrina will be adjusting the schedules accordingly. Also keep in mind that special education students MUST be in your room during direct instruction time for Reading, Math and Language Arts. The inclusion time that Katrina spends inside of your room does not count toward this maximum.*
>
> *Keith Day is the exception to this rule and is classified in the "21–60 percent outside of the regular education classroom" category. He must be pulled out from 75 to 216 minutes per day.*

Bill Bellkoe distributed this letter to all of the B. C. Patanjali Elementary School teachers who had a special education student in their classroom. Actually, Lisa Vans was the only teacher who violated the special education regulations. The other teachers in B. C. Patanjali minimized the students' time with me because they had a true concern for the amount of instruction missed in the regular education classroom. Perhaps Lisa Vans did not feel singled out when Bill Bellkoe distributed this memo to everyone—but she should have felt singled out because she was the only guilty teacher who took advantage of my kindness toward the children.

Only a few school days had passed between the time when Lisa and I had received the memo and therefore had been instructed to follow a specific schedule limiting my time with these children and increasing their time in her classroom. A meeting for Tim Bella had been requested by the school psychologist. The school psychologist had in informed me that Tim Bella had tested out of Special Education. Many professionals, including Shelly Mitchel, Bill Bellkoe, Lisa Vans, and the B. C. Patanjali guidance counselor, were invited to this meeting. The school psychologist announced the latest achievement scores and informed the group of professionals and the parents that Tim Bella no longer needed special education services. At one point during the meeting, the B. C. Patanjali guidance counselor asked Lisa Van's a question: "Tim Bella has spent most of his time with you this year, hasn't he?" Lisa replied "Yes, he has!" I wanted to scream, "How dare you take any credit for Tim's progress!" She out and out lied! She could take no credit for anything that Tim had learned—I had worked so hard with him. Once a child had tested out of special education, he or she no longer needed an IEP. This meant that during the last month of school, Tim Bella would stay in Lisa Vans's classroom 100% percent of the time!

I quickly informed Diane Ridgedan of the situation. Diane asked me, "Who does Tim have, *her*?" as she looked toward Lisa's classroom. I told her yes—unfortunately Tim would spend his last few weeks of fourth grade with Lisa Vans! Diane Ridgedan instructed me to prepare a modified IEP just to keep Tim Bella under my wing until the end of the current academic year. Diane told me what to write in the IEP, to have Mrs. Bella sign it, and to tell Lisa that Tim would continue to come to my room for Math and Reading each day.

Diane had never given me bad advice—except for this! Although Marcel Nulldick was well aware that Tim Bella had tested out of special education and that Diane had instructed on the preparation of this modified document, he held this against me. He falsified information and twisted this around. I really don't know how the man slept at night. Here I was doing what was best for the child, while creating extra work for myself each day—and it was twisted and falsified and held against me! I just continued to ask God why I had to live through such professional adversity. What lessons did God want me to learn from this? Why was I being tortured by tyrants like Brenda Craiger and Marcel Nulldick?

Later, I saw the school psychologist, who was in on the sabotage, and I questioned him. I reminded him that the IEP meeting to dismiss Tim Bella from special education was requested and guided by him based on Tim's most recent diagnostic achievement test scores. The school psychologist replied, "Well, the scores were misleading." After this remark I knew Marcel Nulldick had shared confidential information regarding my dismissal with the school psychologist. Furthermore, Shelly Mitchel knew this too because she was part of the IEP team was and in attendance at the meeting, when the school psychologist dismissed Tim Bella from special education. All information regarding the confidential paper work of Tim Bella had been misconstrued by Marcel Nulldick. The school psychologist and Shelly Mitchel were both in on this segment of the sabotage!

Weak Union

I went to lunch with Gay Pick over Christmas break. She had already known about Dr. Lurk getting fired. We talked about my situation, and she informed me that the Souless Area School District had a weak union. I should have asked for a union representative to accompany me at these ITAP meetings. I went to see the union president on April 26, 2004, at 7:30 AM on a Monday morning. As I was getting out of my car on the very cold morning, I saw Dr. James Ryan get out of his car and walk into district office. The building where I was meeting the Union President and the district office were adjacent to one another. Dr. Ryan did not see me. I wondered if he really knew how vile the actions of Brenda Craiger were. After all, Dr. Lurk had gotten fired, and I was going to get fired—why couldn't Brenda Craiger get fired too? She deserved to be dismissed because she was downright inept.

I had previously contacted the PSEA (Pennsylvania State Education Association) Union President and had given him copies of the documentation that I had accumulated thus far during the academic year. He had had time to review these documents prior to our scheduled meeting on Aril 26, 2004. I felt that he most likely did not bother to read through the documents thoroughly. His words to me were: "Brenda Craiger has a vendetta against you, but there is nothing I can do about it." These were the words of the PSEA Union President for the district. I had paid my union dues, which were several hundred dollars per academic year. The PSEA Union was supposed to protect my job—not take the side of the tyrant, Brenda Craiger. I knew that Marcel Nulldick had warned the Union President that he should choose his words carefully when he spoke to me. I wanted my union dues back—my job was never protected! If this union president was getting paid for his services as Union President, he was cheating PSEA because he did *not* help me! Union representatives were paid to help teachers during times of professional adversity! He should have volunteered to attend all of my ITAP and Friday afternoon meetings with Brenda Craiger.

On Friday, March 26, 2004, Brenda Craiger kept me in her office of torture until 4:45 PM—almost one hour past my contracted time. On that specific day she was nitpicking more than ever. She complained and blatantly lied about my data collection, she said my students were making no progress, and she said my lesson plans did not meet district requirements. This minute and unjustified criticism of me—when I had been working endless hours on my personal time—was out of control! I finally spoke up to the bitch! "You are nitpicking! You have never been fair to me! You would love to see me fired from this place!"

The ITAP Meetings

These meetings were a big joke and a waste of time! ITAP is an acronym for Intensive Teacher Assistance Program. Brenda Craiger always sat at the head of the table because she controlled the axis of evil. She wrote pages of documentation about petty details—most of them based on lies or things that she had intentionally misconstrued. Sometimes I left these meetings crying, and sometimes I left them laughing because they were outrageous! I found it interesting to observe the behavior of Brenda Craiger because she twisted and turned everything I did! These meetings simply gave Brenda Craiger another channel in which to document lies regarding my professional demeanor! Everyone knew I was getting fired in June, —so why waste our time? Ironically, the ITAP meetings did not start until after I informed Marcel Nulldick of the negligent actions that had occurred in Brenda Craiger's building. I was responsible for going three places in one day, which was ridiculous in itself! However, I only attended ITAP meetings in the Mountclair Elementary Building, by the request of Brenda. My work at B. C. Patanjali was proficient without ITAP meetings! The ITAP team included Brenda Craiger, Marcel Nulldick, Shelly Mitchel, Diane Ridgedan, and of course me! (Thank God they allowed Diane Ridgedan to be part of these meetings! She always wanted justice!) Shelly Mitchel, now the actual supervisor of special education for the Souless Area School District, began to think highly of me. I visualized her telling Marcel Nulldick, behind my back that the district really did not want to get rid of a good person like me! However, Marcel Nulldick, finding it necessary to cover the actions of Brenda Craiger, knew that he must fire me!

The preparation of documents on my part and on the part of Brenda

Craiger was outrageous! Rather than spending my time planning lessons for my students, I had to spend a ludicrous amount of time gathering things and making copies for the ludicrous ITAP meetings. Brenda Craiger would spend hours writing documents of sabotage so that she was prepared to make me look bad at each meeting. Then we had to agree on a time when all five busy professionals could meet. This was insane that so much time and energy was spent when everyone knew that I was going to get fired. The preparation for each ITAP meeting diminished the value of each day. It was so frustrating because there were so many positive ways to spend the time in the day, so many positive things to do with your energy that could have a positive outcome. I wanted to do something worthwhile—something that would make my students learn more or help me become a better teacher. ITAP meetings were a total waste of time and energy for everyone involved!

As Gothe said, "Nothing should be prized more highly than the value of each day."

Brenda Craiger wrote endless pages about what a terrible teacher I was: my lesson plans were not up to district standards, my students were not learning enough, and she twisted and turned everything I did. She misconstrued everything! All of my positive accomplishments with my students were twisted and turned against me. She wrote lie after lie, documenting every one of her lies into lengthy documentation. Go Brenda Craiger! Brenda's paperwork was very well documented!

Brenda Craiger informed me on March 5, 2004, that my lesson plans should include the listing of one Reading Mastery lesson per day. I informed Brenda Craiger that the lessons had gotten longer and that it was almost possible to do so with my low-level reading students. The conniving principal stated, "I don't care if you are able to cover one lesson per day—I still want you to write that in your weekly lesson plans." When Brenda Craiger made this statement to me, I sensed the wrongfulness and saw through her phoniness. However, I did what she had told me to do.

If only I had had a Union Representative present when she made this statement. After having professional conversations with Jone Castle, Diane Ridgedan, and Bill Bellkoe, all of which had earned a teaching certificate as a Reading Specialist, I was well aware that rushing these children through daily lessons, when they had not mastered the vocabulary and comprehension questions, was just wrong! It made the students frustrated! In addition, I frequently talked with the two Reading Specialists at B. C. Patanjali Elementary School, seeking advice so that I could better improve my reading instruction for all of my students. I tried to explain this to Brenda Craiger over and over. She was not a Reading Specialist and had never taught scripted reading to learning-disabled students. I turned in my lesson plans following this directive from Brenda Craiger.

At the May 19, 2004, ITAP meeting, in her phony vindictive voice she stated "I have a concern. I have noted that Katrina has listed one lesson per day on her lesson plans, however she is only covering two and one-half lessons per week." I wanted to call her a dishonest bitch! I spoke up to defend myself because she had misconstrued things! This was why a union representative should have accompanied me during my weekly meetings! I reminded her that on 3/5/2004 she had specifically directed me to list one lesson per day on my lesson plans—even though I knew I could not cover the lengthy lessons.!

I told Diane Ridgedan how Brenda Craiger had connived and turned my detailed lesson plans against me. She directed me to document the details and send them to all members of the ITAP team. I did so and submitted the following letter to Dr. Marcel Nulldick.

5/19/2004
Re: Response To ITAP Meeting of 5/18/2004
Dear Dr. Nulldick,
During our meeting of 5/18/04, Mrs. Craiger announced that I had listed one lesson per day on my Reading Mastery Lesson Plans. Previously, I had handed in lesson plans listing only four lessons per week. During our Friday meeting of 3/5/04, Mrs. Craiger informed me that I should list one lesson per day in my plans. I had informed Mrs. Craiger that my reason for having four lessons per week was due to the fact that this was actually what I was able to cover. I informed Mrs. Craiger that I was not able to cover five lessons per week. She told me to plan for five lessons—therefore I changed my plans, even though I knew it was unrealistic to move so quickly.
Following this Friday meeting of 3/5/2004, when I was kept at Mountclair Elementary until 4:45 PM, my lesson plans have listed one lesson per day. I made this change on my lesson plans at the request of Mrs. Craiger.
Sincerely,
Katrina Hall
Cc:
Shelly Mitchel

Diane Ridgedan
Brenda Craiger

When I submitted this documentation of truth and defense to Dr. Marcel Nulldick, on 5/19/2004 I attached copies of my lesson plans prior to the Friday, March 5, 2004, meeting with Brenda Craiger, and copies of my lesson plans written after my March 5 meeting, in which I was following the conniving directive of Brenda Craiger. This situation was similar to the scenario in which Brenda Craiger, in front of Dr. Marcel Nulldick, told me refer to my reading groups as Reading Groups, which I had originally done. I feel that Brenda Craiger behaved this way, in many instances, because she had nothing negative to say about my work, so she twisted and misconstrued my positive accomplishments in an attempt to make me appear incompetent in front of Dr. Marcel Nulldick, Assistant Superintendent.

During the ITAP meeting of May 18, 2004, Marcel Nulldick questioned me. He asked me about a specific IEP, if I had help writing it, to describe the standards that I had used to prepare this IEP, to define baseline data, and many other questions—as if he were interviewing me. (Later, I learned that it was illegal for an administrator to question me.) I was so frustrated by the end of this ITAP meeting. Dr. Marcel Nulldick asked me if Kara, my mentor, helped me prepare an IEP that I had been recently working on! I informed the ITAP team, "I did not ask anyone for help, and I did not tell anyone I was typing Aaron's IEP; I typed it myself!" I finally spoke up and informed the ITAP team, "I am tired of spending my Sundays working for a district from which I am getting fired." I was so frustrated with everything. The ITAP meetings were consistently disconcerting to me, but this one was exceptionally disconcerting!

I asked Dr. Nulldick to meet with me, and he did so on Thursday, May 20, 2004, at B. C. Patanjali Elementary School, prior to the arrival of the students. Marcel Nulldick made the following comment. "I do not understand your frustration level." How could he not understand—he knew Brenda Craiger was twisting, misconstruing, sabotaging, undermining— because I had documented everything. He knew Bertha Both had given herself a huge break at my expense. He was well aware that I been taken advantage of with an unreasonable work load. The only thing that he did not know was that I was in the same boat domestically. School day after school day I watched Bertha Both relax while I did her work; at home, evening after evening, I watched my husband relax while I did all the work! Weekends were no different from school days. Saturday was laundry, errands, dishwasher, bed sheets, and as much cleaning as I could fit in. On Sunday I was back at B. C. Patanjali Elementary School, alone in the building working on my lesson plans, IEPs, and preparation for Brenda's ITAP meetings. I didn't have fifteen minutes to myself—ever!

On Thursday, May 20, 2004, I spoke with Dr. Marcel Nulldick. He was always friendly in person—when he was not with Brenda Craiger—and he smiled a lot. On this day his words to me were, "I don't understand your frustration level." I assume that we all bring our personal selves into our careers. I had received more that my share of the workload—not only in this job but in all jobs, and at home. I was fed up with watching others have free time and an easy life at my expense! My life both professionally and domestically was a treadmill—and Marcel Nulldick wondered why my frustration level was so high.

Field Trip—May 2004

The laziness of Bertha Both amazed me. The special education students were invited to a picnic and day of outdoor activities set up at the elementary building in which Kara worked. Because Bertha and I shared the same students, we both needed to agree to attend. I was so excited to have a different day; and that different day meant fun for my B. C. Patanjali students, and I got to spend an entire day spent with them. When I mentioned this day to Bertha Both, she said she was not going to go because it would be "too much work to keep track of all of those students. It will just be easier for me if I stay here!" After the easy academic year that she had given herself at my expense, she was going to make those students miss a day of fun outdoor activities! If Bertha didn't attend, then I couldn't attend because I would be responsible for instructing the reading groups.

During a casual conversation, Dr. Marcel Nulldick asked me if I was going to take my B. C. Patanjali students to this field trip. I explained to him that Bertha was not going to attend, though I still wanted to take my B. C. Patanjali children. I explained to him that I was going to ask Shelly Mitchel if I could attend, supervising my B. C. Patanjali children, while Bertha Both remained back at Mountclair Elementary. Low and behold, the lazy Bertha changed her mind! After this casual conversation with Dr. Marcel Nulldick, Bertha Both was advised to take her Mountclair special education students on this field trip. Yes, this was extra work for her. She actually had to do something—she was required to prepare permission slips signed by each parent, providing instructions on packing a bagged lunch and packing sunscreen. She was also responsible for an entire day of supervising *all* the Mountclair special education students who had attended the trip! She almost made those children miss out on a fun day, which was really unfair to them. I had grown fond of my Mountclair reading students, and they enjoyed my classes. They were learning to be better readers, and I knew that I was helping them! Lazy Bertha Both had instructed so few children during the 2003–2004 academic year that I wondered if she ever felt that she had not accomplished anything? She was subversive and just didn't care—she was in the wrong profession! Just as Brenda Craiger had told me one day after I told her how late I had stayed at B. C. Patanjali to work, "It's not a job for the lazy!" However, in a school of favorites, some teachers got away with severe laziness!

May 2004

On May 21, 2004 I attended Bill Bellkoe's retirement party. He had worked for thirty-five years in the Souless Area School District along with his wife. Both of his biological children had attended and graduated from the Souless Area School District. He must have felt some dedication to this district. I know he thought highly of me—but he had informed me early on that his opinion of me would not carry much weight. He had explained that due to his retirement, his high opinion of me would be that of a lame duck! I wondered if Bill Bellkoe had *not* been retiring at the end of the 2003 – 2004 academic year, would my situation have changed? Kara, my mentor, once informed me "Well, Brenda Craiger can't fire you from B. C. Patanjali Elementary School!"

On Wednesday, May 26, 2004, I was observed by Dr. Marcel Nulldick. The observation was scheduled late in the academic year due to Dr. Nulldick's eye surgery. Everything went well—the students were well behaved, the lesson was great, and the students were engaged from start to finish. I made a poster for the wall on the open-closed syllable. I also made the same drawing for the table on construction paper so that the students could have a hands-on activity. Dr. Marcel Nulldick liked what he saw. He complimented me on the poster, the hands-on activity, and the controlled behavior of the students. I returned to B. C. Patanjali and told Bill how well things had gone. Bill replied, "Well good! Then maybe he will feel guilty." I wonder if Dr. Marcel Nulldick felt guilty when he fired me.

My lesson included a poster and example of the open-closed syllable. I selected specific examples for the poster and the hands-on activity because those specific examples were not on my quiz. Even though Dr. Marcel Nulldick complimented my use of the poster and the hands-on activity, he went home and talked with his wife, who also was a special education teacher, and found a way to write something negative in the observation summary. He lied to me! He questioned my specific examples on the poster, and I told him I had intentionally used those specific examples because I did not want to put quiz questions and answers on the poster. I had planned to keep the poster up on the wall in Bertha Both's classroom until the last day of school. I had reasons for the content and specific examples listed on my poster. He told me he would not use my examples against me when he prepared his written documentation of my formal clinical observation form. However, when I read the negative evaluation, he had used it against me! Surprise! Surprise! Why would I be surprised that I was lied to once again by an administrator in the Souless Area School District? How did this man sleep at night? It is no wonder that he sounded as though he was having a nervous breakdown when he spoke in public—it was the manifestation of guilt due to acting as Brenda Craiger's accomplice in my victimization and sabotage.

On Wednesday, May 26, 2004, in the afternoon Dr. Marcel Nulldick observed me at Mountclair Elementary Building. Simultaneously, B. C. Patanjali Elementary School was having their end-of-the-year field day. I so much wanted to stay at B. C. Patanjali that day and watch the students that I had worked with all year participate in the fun outdoor activities. I watched the groups of students and teachers in their matching yellow T-shirts. I could not stop thinking about how things would have gone if Mountclair had not been part of my schedule.

Bill's Retirement Party

Bill's retirement party was beautiful. Of course Brenda Craiger did not attend because they hated one another. All of the B. C. Patanjali teachers were present, and Bill was dancing with his wife and really enjoying himself! I wore a white dress and summer blazer, for which I received many compliments. I watched Dr. Marcel Nulldick drink large amounts of alcohol, and I overheard a conservation between Dr. Nulldick's wife and another B. C. Patanjali teacher, learning that Dr. Nulldick had a favorite kind of whiskey, among several additional alcoholic favorites. I felt sorry for Dr. Marcel Nulldick, Assistant Superintendent, because if was as dependent upon alcohol as his wife had admitted, then he was an alcoholic! I know drinking alcohol zaps you physically. If one weakens oneself physically, one also weakens oneself metaphysically. For example, people who meditate are more in touch with themselves spiritually; therefore they no longer desire to feel good through the consumption of alcohol. They perceive alcohol as something that makes them feel bad, not good. Apparently, Dr. Marcel Nulldick was far away from a spiritual existence, like most of the individuals that I had come into contact with at the Souless Area School District. Dr. Marcel Nulldick thought that a spiritual existence was making an appearance in a church where religious dogma was presented every Sunday, carrying your Bible, sitting beside your best friend Beach, and being upset if the familiar minister is absent that week. It is just a show, nothing more or less. After all, this was an appearance, not a true spiritual existence!

I watched people ruin their health with alcohol and I thought how sad it was. Once again, I realized the pleasure that I had experienced because I had outgrown my desire to consume alcohol. I was more in touch with my physical existence and my metaphysical existence. They all drank a lot! The only person I had befriended in this school district who did not consume alcohol was Diane Ridgedan. I was disappointed when she did not attend Bill Bellkoe's retirement party, because I would have enjoyed sharing the evening with a friend.

My Last Encounters with the Tyrant Brenda Craiger

I unfortunately had to meet with the tyrant, Brenda Craiger, every Friday after school, from 3:20 PM to sometimes almost 5:00 PM. During the last week of May, 2004, I planned to go to the dreaded office of Brenda Craiger on May 28th, 2004, because May 28th was a Friday and that was our scheduled meeting time. I checked my mailbox at Mountclair Elementary school on a daily basis. When I arrived at Mountclair on Friday, May 28, 2004, I went directly to Bertha Both's classroom. After I finished instructing scripted reading to my three back-to-back groups, I walked to the faculty mailbox. The mailbox was located in front of Brenda Craiger's office. I looked inside the mailbox and found a note dated May 25,2004! She even lied about the date she wrote the note. If someone checked the carbon copies of her memo book, they could easily prove that she wrote the note on 5/28/2004 and she placed it in my mailbox on 5/28/2004. The note read, "I will not be meeting with you on May 28. Enjoy your weekend and holiday." Why would she lie about the date? I know she placed that memo note in my mailbox on Friday the 28th, because I checked my mailbox every single day. I know why she canceled—because Dr. Marcel Nulldick told her to stop torturing me. He told her this because he did not want me to quit so near the end of the year due to a nervous breakdown caused by Brenda Craiger. He told her to stop! It took him long enough—she tortured me from the start, and now that the year was over, he told her to stop.

On Thursday, June 3, 2004, I was walking toward the copier, which was located near Brenda Craiger's office. Brenda Craiger was standing adjacent to the faculty mailbox area having a conversation with someone. I walked by them—not extremely close—but I could see the tyrant out of the corner of my eye. It was odd, because I actually did not notice her just standing there. There was no need for her to move because I had plenty of walking space to get to the copier. Brenda Craiger stopped in the middle of her conversation with another person and said, "Katrina, excuse me." The phony kindness that existed in her tone, as she emphasized the syllables in my name, was outrageous. The phony sound of her voice made me want to vomit! I was nowhere near her—it was very odd. I did not acknowledge her—I did not look at her, I did not utter a word, —I just ignored her—I pretended she did not exist! This was the most hurtful thing I could do from a psychological perspective. The developmental psychologists have taught us that positive attention is the best type of interaction between parent and child, that negative interaction is second, and that even negative attention is better that no attention and no interaction. Hopefully she felt resentment because I did not acknowledge her presence and her existence! I did not even look at her. I totally ignored her existence! And that was the last time I ever saw Brenda Craiger!

Federal Court

I had hoped to take the facts in this book to federal court if necessary. However, the PSEA lawyer that I paid to represent me took my money and did not even read my reports and documentation of professional misconduct. To add to this frustration, a renowned psychic medium informed me on two separate occasions that if I would take this situation into litigation, I would win and the outcome would be positive. Winning a legal case, based on the facts in this book, would be an expected manifestation of my detailed documentation. This book has documented only a fraction of the sabotage and undermining that I endured during the 2003–2004 academic year. I can visualize Brenda Craiger and Dr. Marcel Nulldick saying, "I swear to tell the truth, the whole truth, and nothing but the truth." Then, I can hear them saying, "I don't recall. I don't recall. I don't recall." The obvious truth is that if they are saying, "I don't recall," they are not telling the truth. They must be dishonest because they do so recall—and I also recall. They can just lie and say they don't recall, but I know the truth, they know the truth, and God knows the truth. Writing this book will help to provide me with some closure, catharsis, and redemption from my 180 days of suffering from the victimization of Brenda Craiger!

PSEA Article

Later, I read an article from the February 2004 PSEA (Pennsylvania State Education Association) *Voice* Newsletter. The article was written by John Audi and specifically stated that if an administrator calls a teacher into a meeting, the teacher does not have to attend unless a Union Representative is available. I should have been informed of this. I paid my union dues during this time of professional adversity. Every Friday afternoon I met with Brenda Craiger—plus those ridiculous ITAP meetings—and always exclusive of any union representation present! Also, it is illegal to question a teacher unless a union representative is present. The article states, "You have the right to remain silent. Anything you say can and will be used against you." It goes on to say, "Every American is familiar with the Miranda warnings read to an accused before police questioning. So, too, should PSEA members know their rights to union representation when called into a meeting for questioning by an administrator.... The Weingarten right comes into play when the meeting is investigatory in nature and when the employee reasonably believes discipline may be imposed. Although it sounds simple enough, there are certain rulings interpreting these elements of which you should be aware." I unequivocally believed that I was going to get fired. This article then states,

> Should an employer deny a clear request for representation and attempt to continue the investigation, the employee is well advised to state that he or she is choosing not to answer any questions without representation.... Just as the criminally accused have the right to an attorney during police questioning, an employee under the Weingarten rule has the right to a union representative during

employer questioning.... It has been ruled in Pennsylvania that employees have the right to union representation during a review of a performance evaluation.... As such, if an employer's infringement results in the imposition of discipline based upon information that it obtained at the unlawful interview, the employer will be required to make that employee whole for any and all losses.

I was so excited when I read this article written by John Audi, renowned PSEA attorney. It is amazing: A teacher has a right to union representation during a performance evaluation! Additionally, Dr. Marcel Nulldick was unlawful when he questioned me during the ITAP meeting of May 18, 2004. I immediately telephoned and e-mailed my PSEA attorney. He never got back to me. Once again he took my money but did nothing to represent me!

All Things Happen for a Reason

Occasionally at Mountclair Elementary, I would bump into a substitute teacher named Mrs. Walters. I had known her from my previous employment as a substitute teacher in the surrounding school districts. On Monday, May 17, 2004, I bumped into her at the copier located near Brenda Craiger's office. I had also bumped into her at B. C. Patanjali Elementary School, and she was not aware that I went to three places within the Souless Area School District in one day. We exchanged hellos and she stated, "You are in the wrong place!" Wow, that was exactly how it felt! God did not want me to work in the Souless Area School District! God wanted me to work in another school district! Later, I told Diane Ridgedan about the statement Mrs. Walters had made, and Diane replied, "She got that right!"

A certain group of teachers in B.C. Patanjali Elementary School held a prayer meeting before homeroom one morning per week. One of the members invited me, although I declined to attend because I was so busy; I asked her to remember me in prayer. She was a friend who was well aware that I was being sabotaged at Montclair Elementary School. During my final weeks of employment, my friend spoke to me about my situation—because at this point, everyone knew I was getting fired. I expressed to her that the only rationale I could come up with for my situation was the fact that God just did not want me to work in this district! God must have wanted me to help people in another school distract—but not this one. She agreed that this was a very good perspective, a good way to look at my employment situation.

A Friend From B. C. Patanjali
Elementary School

Bonnie Clark, a friend of mine at B. C. Patanjali, provided me with a letter of recommendation, which I added to my credential file.

Bonnie's letter stated the following:

June 15, 2004

To Whom It May Concern:
   Katrina Hall worked as a learning support teacher at B. C. Patanjali Elementary School in the 2003–2004 school year. During this time Katrina worked with my third grade students both in and out of the classroom. She also worked with me in an inclusion setting two times a week.
   Katrina showed enthusiasm for her job. She put in long hours to accomplish her goals. While working with the students, she always displayed a positive, encouraging demeanor. My students were eager to attend her classes.
   When faced with challenges in her first year of teaching, Katrina was willing to seek help. She was open to ideas and suggestions. Sincerely,

Bonnie Clark

That letter was written on June 15, 2004, and was sent to me immediately. Somehow this letter got by Marcel Nulldick. Soon after I received this letter from Bonnie Clark, I sent her a request to complete a recommendation form for my application to graduate school. First of all, it took forever for her to submit it back to me, and second, when it came the recommendation was so negative that I tossed it and went to other sources to have these forms completed. When this happened, like a movie with bad cops, I knew exactly what had happened. Marcel Nulldick had gotten to her too! Marcel Nulldick had informed Bonnie Clark to have no contact with me if she wanted to keep her job! And of course, because we all need our jobs to keep a roof over our heads and pay taxes and keep food on the table, Bonnie Clark was forced to listen to him.

In August 2004, Marcel Nulldick screwed me out of getting hired in several different school districts. Also in August, 2004, Marcel Nulldick also instructed Bonnie Clark not to recommend me to graduate school. I sent Bonnie a few purple forms that I needed in order to apply to graduate school. The remarks on the purple forms were unequivocally skewed under the supervision of Marcel Nulldick. Marcel Nulldick told all of my friends in the Souless School District to have no contact with me. I had several friends at B. C. Patanjali Elementary School, including Bonnie Clark, Kara Keep, Diane Ridgedan, and Jan Hatfield (an old friend whom I had known for years as a substitute teacher). In addition, Marcel Nulldick told Gay Pick to have no contact with me. Jan Hatfield and I went way back—we had our daughters in Brownies and Girl Scouts together. I knew her children from substitute teaching, and she knew my children from working in the local middle school. We were friends and often went out to lunch together. I treated.

As for Gay Pick and I, although we had not known each other for many years, we were also friends. We too had lunch together. I treated, and Gay Pick replied, "I will get it next time." Well, next time never came because Marcel Nulldick told all of these people to have no contact with me, and they listened. Jan Hatfield and the others who continued to work in the Souless Area School District had a reason to listen to Marcel Nulldick—but Gay Pick had no reason. First of all, she was an administrator in another district. Second, she thought highly of me when we were taking our graduate courses together. Gay Pick must have had dinner with Marcel Nulldick, at which my confidential dismissal was discussed. Two summers following my dismissal from the Souless Area School District, I bumped into her in a local shopping center. I said hello and we exchanged greetings. I instinctively knew that Gay had spoken with Marcel Nulldick and that he must have said negative things about me. He must have told her that I was incompetent because she asked me: "What are you teaching, life skills?" I informed her that I was teaching English to fifty-two students who had an IEP and that I simultaneously had a case load of twenty-two students. I knew during our conversation that Marcel had said negative things about me and that he had instructed Gay to have no contact with me.

August 2004

Thanks to Marcel Nulldick, my many successful interviews were completed to no avail. He gave me a negative reference numerous times. However, I was not about to give up! I recall one of our last conversations in which Marcel Nulldick told me that I needed to "get a fresh start in a new district." He should have informed me that he would do everything in his power to prevent me from getting that fresh start to which he had referred! I decided that I would complete my Master's in Special Education at a state university during the 2004–2005 academic year. Fortunately, with the undergraduate courses that I had previously completed, I was able to complete this degree in one year.

As spring of 2005 approached, I began to send out my credentials once again. Although I did not have satisfactory observations for the Spring of my last year of employment, I did have an excellent observation from October 2003 and a letter written by Bill Bellkoe in June 2004. Also, feeling that I could trust Bill, I wrote to him in March 2005 so that I could have an accurate telephone number to list, to use Bill as a reference. The letter read as follows:

> *March 02, 2004*
> *Dear Bill;*
> *I hope you and Carol are enjoying your time and relaxing a lot. I have several interviews scheduled, and need to know if I can continue to use you as a reference. I have enclosed a copy of the following letter with my credential packet.*
> *I have recently attempted to telephone you at the home number listed on your letter of reference. I have attempted to contact you to*

*confirm the fact that I have continued to list you as a reference and
to find a way to have the schools contact you. However, I have been
unable to reach you. Therefore, the schools will have no way to contact
you.*

*Please let me know where I stand with using you as a reference. I
have recently updated REAP and Standard, and I have listed you as a
reference, using the home telephone number provided in your letter.*

*My home telephone number is (123)456-1044. Thanks so
much.*

Fondly,
Katrina Hall

Bill Bellkoe telephoned me and supplied me with an accurate telephone
number. I was grateful for this and was happy to hear that I could use him as
a reference. I sent credential packets to the same districts that I had during
the spring and summer of 2004. I did not hear back from them—nothing!
It was amazing how the lies of one dishonest administrator can result in
professional suicide. If I could change one thing about the public school
system, it would be to require them to video record all teacher observations
and submit this video to PDE (the Pennsylvania Department of Education)
with the required paperwork. One PSEA lawyer informed me, "You think
this only happened to you—it happens all the time. Sabotage! Favoritism!
Unethical and unprofessional behaviors! Pettiness!" Another attorney
informed me, "You must remember, any administrator could take the
best teachers in the world and do this to them." If these statements made
by experienced lawyers are true, then why have we not changed the laws? I
have learned from one lawyer that teachers are fired because administrators
falsify information, but administrators can get away with murder and
never lose their job unless they have sexually harassed a student or sold
illegal substances! Something needs to change! How is it that these codes of
conduct can be violated over and over by any administrator, and nothing is
done? If administrators were required to submit a video tape of all teacher
observations, they could no longer provide negative evaluations simply
because they did not like a certain teacher.

Administrators have so much power to improve things! Instead of
falsifying information regarding hard-working teachers, they could put
their energy into something positive. They could work on implementing
parenting skills courses for future parents of senior high students. I will
never understand why our teenagers are not taught positive parenting

techniques through public education! They could work on implementing a state mandated nutrition curriculum with the goal of reducing adolescent obesity. Administrators have the power to make a positive change to help develop emotionally sound and physically healthy adolescents in our society.

Rather than creating an altruistic change in public education, I observed Brenda Craiger putting a great deal of time and energy into the perjury of many educator misconduct codes. It bothered me that the energy expenditure was consistently negative due to the vileness of Brenda Craiger. I wanted to be part of the positive change which a public education can create in a student's life—I did not want to be part of those ridiculous ITAP meetings!

Fired!
June 2, 2004

On June 2, 2004, I was driving my 1988 Toyota Celica out the back roads toward B. C. Patanjali Elementary School. The DJ announced the morning weather report, saying, "After today there will be sunny days ahead!" On that day, Marcel Nulldick fired me! He also informed me that I needed to write him a letter stating that I had resigned from my position. He added the fact that if I did not write the letter of resignation, he would list my name in the newspaper as being fired. Both Diane Ridgedan and Bill Bellkoe encouraged me to promptly write the letter. If I had gotten fired, I would never get hired again! If Marcel Nulldick had not consistently told his administrative friends and acquaintances not to hire me, I would have gotten hired during the 2004–2005 academic year! On this day Diane Ridgedan stayed with me in the conference room while Marcel Nulldick fired me! She didn't have to do this, but she chose to do so. Of course, I was emotionally upset as Marcel read lie after lie as premise for my getting dismissed from my position. After Marcel Nulldick left the room, Diane hugged me while I cried. Diane Ridgedan was literally a shoulder to cry on! What a special person she was—I was for 180 days so very grateful for her friendship, emotional support, continual kindness, and professional guidance. Diane referred to Brenda Craiger as a "bitch!". Diane was always so proper and such a person of integrity that it was difficult to believe that she would ever say anything negative about anyone—even Brenda Craiger! I asked Diane Ridgedan why Brenda Craiger didn't attend this meeting in which I was being fired by Marcel Nulldick. I figured that Brenda would enjoy this, listening to the falsified, documented reasons for my dismissal!

She told me that I would not have to worry about bumping into Brenda today because she had gone to the zoo. If fact the entire school (Mountclair Elementary went—even that tyrant of a principal, Brenda Craiger!) Diane Ridgedan consoled me and said, "At least you don't have to go *over there* [Mountclair Elementary] today!" I told Diane Ridgedan that I hoped Brenda Craiger would get bitten by an alligator or a tiger and I hoped she would get rabies! That was the last in-person conversation I had with Diane Ridgedan. It saddens me to think about this.

The day after I was fired, Bill Bellkoe and I had a casual conversation in his B. C. Patanjali office. Bill informed me, "Everyone has a rough first year, but yours has been exceptionally rough!" Somehow this comment did not ease the emotional turmoil of this academic year. Somehow "exceptionally rough" was a significant understatement!

I thought that Diane Ridgedan and I would remain lifelong friends because our friendship during the 2003–2004 academic year had grown. We talked frequently during the summer of 2004 because she was well aware that Dr. Marcel Nulldick was providing negative verbal references to his administrative friends in surrounding school districts. Although we talked during that summer, I know she was instructed by Dr. Marcel Nulldick to have no further contact with me. I know she did not answer my e-mails and telephone calls because she financially needed her job.

On June 4, 2004, I wrote the letter, just as I had been directed to do. It was short and sweet!

June 04, 2004
Souless Area School District
12345 North Hell Road
Oneville, PA 66666

Dear Dr. Nulldick,

I have decided to resign from my position as Special Education Teacher for the Souless Area School District.

Sincerely,
Katrina Hall

It was short and sweet, and that was that. After 180 days of torture, I was instructed to write a letter of resignation! Brenda Craiger should have been instructed to resign because she was a liar and an inept, unethical administrator! Dr. Marcel Nulldick should have been instructed to write a letter of resignation because he was a liar and sounded like he was having a nervous breakdown whenever he spoke in public. Bertha Both should have been instructed to write a letter of resignation because she was a fat liar and an extremely lazy, unethical person.

I hand delivered my letter to Dr. Marcel Nulldick on Thursday, June 4, 2004. I also needed to clear up things in the benefits office. When I walked in I knew that the clerical workers in district office were well aware that I had gotten fired. I sensed it and experienced strong feelings of their negative awareness of my situation. It was a very small district, and the Central Office was small too. Everyone knew! The clerical workers knew, the janitors knew, the administrators knew, the teachers knew. The entire backwoods town of Oneville knew that I had gotten fired!

Brenda Craiger and Marcel Nulldick had tortured me and lied about my performance on numerous occasions. Bertha Both took advantage of a new teacher to the district. The sabotage and undermining was consistent during the 180 days of my employment at the Souless Area School District. Dr. Wayne Dyer tells us, "Human beings who do damage or inflict pain on anybody else are far greater victims than those they victimize, and must answer to a law of the universe for all those things." I just know that I would rather be me, fired and jobless, than Brenda Craiger and Marcel Nulldick and Bertha Both. I am glad I am me! I wonder how much harm they have bestowed upon themselves. Several pieces of literature teach us that the negative lyrics from music can make cause illness both mentally and physically. If listening to negative lyrics can harm us, I wonder what the behaviors that I have witnessed, and have defended myself against in this school district, have done to Brenda Craiger, Marcel Nulldick, and Berth Both. They must answer to a higher power! They know they have lied; I know they have lied; and God knows they have lied!

Regretfully Accepted

Ironically enough, I received a letter from Dr. James Ryan, Superintendent of The Souless Area School District. The letter stated:

June 15, 2004
Ms. Katrina Hall
1234 Upper Valley Road
Pleasantburg, PA 12345
Dear Ms. Hall:
 The Board of School Directors, at their June 14, 2004, meeting, regretfully accepted your resignation as a professional at the B. C. Patanjali Elementary School, effective at the end of the 2003-2004 school year.
 On behalf of the Board, thank you for your service to the Souless Area School District.
Sincerely,
James Ryan, EdD
Superintendent
Am
Cc: Mr. Bill Bellkoe
Business Office

Of course, I laughed when I read this! Unbelievable! Incredible! The school board of directors "regretfully accepted" my resignation? Was Dr. Marcel Nulldick present while they "regretfully accepted" my resignation? Was Mrs. Brenda Craiger present when they "regretfully accepted" my resignation? Lie upon lie upon lie! Excuse me, I was *not* dismissed from, nor did I resign from, B. C. Patanjali Elementary School! B. C. Patanjali was the positive, productive, wonderful part of my professional day. I was dismissed from Mountclair Elementary because the principal, Brenda Craiger, hated me. And she hated me because she hated Bill Bellkoe, and she hated me because Bill Bellkoe and I had a positive, professional rapport!

During the academic year, while attending a districtwide in-service, on Monday, February 16, 2004, I bumped into an old friend whom I had known from my work as a substitute in another local school district. She and I had our daughters in the same Girl Scout troop. Additionally, we worked in the same building—I as a long-term substitute and she was a permanent teacher. In late June I had lunch with this friend, Janie Ton, who was currently employed at the Souless Area School District. Janie informed me that she had read in the local newspaper that four teachers were dismissed from the Souless Area School District due to their failure to complete the necessary college credits. Janie asked me over lunch if I needed to complete more college credits to remain certified. I informed Janie that this certainly was *not* the case! This was honestly a bunch of pathetic lies in the local newspaper! Perhaps three of the four dismissed/resigned teachers were in need of certification through earning additional college credits, but not me! No, I left because Brenda Craiger hated me!

Later, during the fall semester of 2004, I tried to contact Janie Ton, who like Diane Ridgedan would not return my calls or my e-mails. I instinctively knew that Dr. Marcel Nulldick had told Janie and Diane to have no further contact with me. These actions, at the insistence of Dr. Martin Nulldick, prove that he is guilty of victimization and lies, and this proves to me that he covered the heinous actions of Brenda Craiger. If Dr. Marcel Nulldick had nothing to hide and nothing to cover up, then there would be no reason for him to tell my friends to have no further contact with me. Covering the actions and behavior of an unethical principal supersedes integrity and honesty in the public school system.

July 2005

I had an interview at a local public school district in Pennsylvania in July 2005. The assistant principal who interviewed me asked me several questions similar to those that I had been researching to prepare for my Master's Comprehensive Examination. As she asked me question after question, I rambled on in detail, spitting out-up-to-date facts about Special Education. Between my one-year experience, my graduate course work, and my upcoming comps, I most likely knew more about Special Education than she. She was impressed with me and I knew it. Then we also had a conversation about our biological children. I told her how much I valued education and that I truly wanted to be a positive role model to my children. I told her I felt it was very positive for my children to see me going back for additional teaching certificates and my Master's Degree—in this way I was a positive role model. I could have been sitting on the couch smoking a cigarette—instead look what I am doing! Look what I am doing with my life right now! The Assistant Principal who interviewed me liked such statements. I knew I was in when I left her office! Now I just had to deal with the infamous spring 2004 observation!

When I left her office, she immediately telephoned Dr. Lett and said, "You'd better get this one before someone else (i.e., another public school district) does!" She told me this later in the school year, during a casual conversation. I also informed her that she had asked questions which I fortunately had recently researched in order to prepare for my graduate comprehensive examination.

Following two more interviews, I was hired by this local public school district. Then one day during the August 2005 Teacher Induction, I received a message asking me to provide my Spring 2004 Teacher Observations from the Souless Area School District. I was distraught! Here I was, hired and halfway through Teacher Induction! I came home and telephoned the PSEA lawyer who really had no advice; however, he took my money and charged me for the time. A couple days passed, and I contacted the secretary at district office and told her it would take me a few days to provide her with my most recent teacher observations. Frankly, I did not know what to say or do! If I actually provided my unsatisfactory and marginal teacher evaluations from Brenda Craiger and Marcel Nulldick, this public school district would renege on my position during teacher induction.

A couple more days passed, and I was ready to provide my falsified unsatisfactory and marginal teacher evaluations to the clerical workers in district office—they had requested them, and I had no choice! I telephoned the appropriate person and told her that I would bring them to her as soon as I was able to locate and copy them. I pretended I was not aware of what she actually needed because I wanted her to think I was on top of requesting such documents from the Souless Area School district. I sent her an e-mail asking, "How many evaluations from each school do you need?" I also informed her, "I don't know if I am able to get any documentation from my previous place of employment." I was stalling and had no idea how to resolve this one; I just prayed. I was well aware that God did not want me to work in the Souless Area School District! I felt positive energy about working for this new public school district and knew that God wanted me to help many students and parents in this school district. I had no ideas what to do—I had been hired! A few more days passed and before I knew it, September 21, 2005, had arrived! On this date I received another e-mail from Dr. Lett's secretary; the subject read, "Satisfactory Evaluations." My heart jumped as a burst of adrenaline entered my bloodstream! Could they renege on my position at this point? She informed me that she only needed two teacher observations. The e-mail read as follows.

> *Semi-annual evaluations are conducted two times a year. That, or a letter from the principal stating performance was satisfactory, is what we required in order to count experience out of our district toward tenure. Therefore, I can use the letter from Mr. Bellkoe to cover 2003–2004. If you would like the experience from the charter school, in which you were previously employed, also to count toward tenure, please provide me with a copy of a satisfactory evaluation for that time period.*

She informed me that she already had a copy of Bill Bellkoe's October 2003 observation and she informed me that my letter of reference from Bill Bellkoe could be used as my spring 2004 teacher observation because it was dated May 25, 2004! Amazing! Utterly Amazing! A letter, just one letter, changed my professional life and my annual income forever! The letter read as follows:

To Whom It May Concern:

Katrina Hall worked as a learning support teacher on a half-day basis in my building during the 2003–2004 school year. She was responsible for instructing eight students with disabilities in reading, math, or both. These students spent up to one hour and fifteen minutes per day in her classroom and received the remainder of their instruction in self-contained classrooms.

Katrina demonstrated strong instructional skills in the use of a balanced reading curriculum designed to supplement and reinforce the program in the regular classroom. She also provided remediation in math to a number of the students.

Her student control was strong, and she maintained a rapport with her students that allowed her to motivate them to do their best for her. She also spent "pull-in" time in each classroom to help her students gain the skills that they needed to succeed in their regular classroom.

During the year, Katrina trained a new aide and supervised her work for three hours each day.

Although this was Katrina's first year of teaching, she showed a great deal of dedication to her job. She came in early and often spent weekends in the building preparing for the next week's instruction.

If you need additional information about this promising new teacher, please do not hesitate to call me at (111) 123-1234. As I am retiring June 30, 2004, I would be happy to speak with you at my home number (111) 567-5678 after that date.

Sincerely,

William Bellkoe

Principal

B. C. Patanjali Elementary School

Financially, this was wonderful. I worked at the Souless Area School District for $36,800 per year. I was entering my newly employed public school district at $45,900 per year! Not only had I moved on, but my move was financially lucrative! In five short years my annual income reached more than $62,000 per year. Just as the DJ on the radio had stated the day I was fired—after today there will be sunny days ahead! The outcome was positive spiritually, as well as financially lucrative. The daily emotional turmoil caused by Brenda Craiger paid off. Brenda Craiger tested my emotional and spiritual strength and I was able to grow stronger. She tried to break me both emotionally and spiritually, but I came through—a little worn, but stronger! Somehow this experience made me a better person because I was a more understanding and more mature adult.

The laws and codes of misconduct are ancient—they need to change! I don't understand why administrators can behave this way and harass a teacher for 180 days and get away with it. One thing that would certainly help is to have all observations videotaped and submitted to PDE (the Pennsylvania Department of Education) so that administrators cannot lie about a teacher's instruction and ability to perform the professional responsibilities required to fulfill the position. The other change that is needed is to have more than a "law clerk" receive a formal complaint. I was able to prove beyond doubt that Brenda Craiger and Martin Nulldick had lied, falsifying fact after fact regarding the details of my performance (and my dismissal) and I submitted those documents to the PDE (Pennsylvania Department of Education). Did the PDE (Pennsylvania Department of Education) ever investigate? Did those people who tortured me also have sleepless nights while the codes of misconduct were being investigated? Did any of those people receive a formal reprimand for their malicious actions?

I spoke to numerous lawyers who informed me, "It happens all time." "You think that you are the only one this has ever happen to." "You must understand that an administrator could do this to the most competent teacher in the world." "Maybe you feel that nothing has been accomplished regarding your situation, however if you have submitted Misconduct Forms to the PDE (Pennsylvania Department of Education) then you have caused those people some sleepless nights." "The law always favors the employer and not the employee, even when the acts are malicious." If such statements are true—then we need to change things. We need to change the law so that the behavior of unethical administrators is not legally overlooked. I will never understand how administrators can get away with such actions of harassment, sabotage, undermining, dishonest documentation of facts, and out and out heinous acts that violate the current teacher's contact—yet no legal action was taken. I asked one PSEA lawyer if he thought that something underhanded had taken place. I was implying that the Souless Area School District had paid off, monetarily, the acting judge at the PDE (Pennsylvania Department of Education). This lawyer replied, "Anything is possible." I would like to know if these reported misconduct forms were filed away by a law clerk because there were no reports of sexual misconduct or drug abuse, as one lawyer implied that this could very well happen. Or were they actually investigated, and therefore at least caused these four hurtful souls some sleepless nights? I may never know the answer to this, but certainly I hope to initiate change. If my 180 days of emotional pain and suffering and professional adversity helps create a legal change, then I have not suffered in vain. I do not want my 180 days of emotional and professional suffering to have been in vain. I want my suffering and my detailed documentation to help teachers who are not as strong as I am.

Professionally, I had divided loyalties. I loved the classroom and I loved my students. I had a burning desire to become a classroom teacher in a public school, and I was determined to fulfill this desire. This was the only career that I had ever considered—and I had known since I was in sixth grade that teaching was my true career calling. I hated the sabotage and undermining that I endured for 180 days. I hated the fact that administrators, specifically Brenda Craiger, could lie and professionally get away with murder!

Main Characters

I know that when you victimize another soul, karma will get you. When you hurt someone else, you only hurt yourself. The hurt and pain that you have caused another soul to suffer will come back to you—it may even be magnified a hundred or a thousand times. You will be karmatically reimbursed for your hurtful actions. Similarly, if you go through your day and your demeanor is one of love and kindness—you treat people in a positive manner because you really want to help another soul—then you will be karmatically reimbursed for your positive actions. This positive reimbursement may be magnified a hundred or a thousand times because this is how our universe works! Any time these big wigs thought that they were getting away with lies and sabotage (on my behalf) they were only hurting themselves. Their magnified hurt could come back to them in numerous ways—not necessarily professionally, but it will come back to haunt them. I know they lied, they know they lied, and God knows they lied. Every thought and action impacts other people, and thoughts are forces in the universe. Brenda Craiger, Marcel Nulldick, and Bertha Both did not get away with anything when they victimized me. As Percy Bysshe Shelly has informed us in "Love's Philosophy":

> —*Nothing in this world is single;*
> *All things by a law divine in each other's being mingle.*

Brenda Craiger is the most hurtful person whom I have ever meant; I wondered if she was from the dark side. When she victimized me, she brought a great deal of harm and suppression upon herself. Brenda Craiger, Principal, of Mountclair Elementary School, is number one on the list of heinous souls. Brenda Craiger made me suffer professionally and emotionally for 180 days! She made me feel as if I were a terrible person—but in reality she was the terrible person. She made me feel that I did not belong in the teaching profession. She told me I was not capable of making professional decisions. In reality, she was not capable of making emotionally intelligent decisions. Every time I left her office or any meeting situation, I would think, "I would rather be me than Brenda Craiger." Every meeting with her was disconcerting to me. I was thankful that I had developed the emotional intelligence and spiritual maturity upon which to base my professional behavior. Brenda Craiger, on the other hand, was in this professional position of power and lacked emotional intelligence; she had never developed spiritual maturity. Every time Brenda Craiger lied to Dr. Marcel Nulldick, she thought she sabotaged me and hurt me, but in reality she was only hurting herself. I was strong enough both emotionally and physically to live through the 2003–2004 academic year. However, others were not. She tortured teachers, and the end result was that of early retirement or resigning due to a nervous breakdown. She did not break me, although she tried! She never killed my spirit or my love for the students, although she tried! She never took away the joy that I experienced when my students told me how much I had helped them learn to become better readers. She never destroyed my burning desire to teach, although she gave it her best effort! I wondered how Brenda Craiger slept at night—she certainly caused me sleepless night after sleepless night! Truly, she tortured me! I know she lied; she knows she lied; and God knows she lied!

Dr. Marcel Nulldick, Assistant Superintendent, is number two on the list of heinous souls. Dr. Marcel Nulldick is a complex person because when I was alone with him, I sensed no negativity; the negative vibes entered the room with Brenda Craiger, not Dr. Nulldick. Dr. Marcel Nulldick was actually genial when I was alone with him, and we shared some friendly conversations. He actually had a kind of altruistic demeanor which I noticed when Brenda Craiger was absent from our meetings. In May 2004, just a few days prior to his "I will fire Katrina" meeting, the secretary of education visited B. C. Patanjali Elementary School. At this time Dr. James Ryan, the Superintendent, was unfortunately out with prostate cancer; therefore, it was Dr. Marcel Nulldick's responsibility to introduce her to the students, parents, and faculty who had gathered in the cafeteria. A large group of people had gathered and were waiting for Dr. Marcel Nulldick to speak! A few moments prior to this introduction, everyone involved had gathered in the elementary school library for prayer.

Coincidentally, I was standing near Dr. Marcel Nulldick and had observed how nervous he looked! He blinked his eyes rapidly and appeared to be extremely nervous! I almost had sympathy for him because he looked so desperately nervous—and then I remembered that he was going to fire me in a few short days, and this thought made the feeling of sympathy turn to a thought of "It serves you right!" The school official leading the group in prayer mentioned that in the near future, the group would be directed to exit the library and enter the cafeteria, at which time Dr. Marcel Nulldick would introduce the secretary of education from PDE (the Pennsylvania Department of Education). I saw him as these words were being spoken: his eyes blinked quickly, and he just looked so nervous; I really felt sorry for him. (I had gotten over my fear of public speaking quickly!) When the time came for Dr. Nulldick to introduce our PDE (Pennsylvania Department of Education) guest, he didn't say anything at first. Then he sort of trembled and said, "Good morning! I would like to introduce you to Ms. Emily Raber, the Secretary of Education." That was it! He was trembling, his voice quivered, and he sounded as though he were about to have a nervous breakdown. He only made a one-sentence statement! The guest looked shocked! However, she took his place behind the pulpit and spoke her piece with confidence. B. C. Patanjali was fortunate to have such a guest! I felt sorry for Dr. Nulldick because he so nervous when it came to public speaking. Maybe, he would suffer in front of a large crowd. Perhaps he would tremble, and his voice would quiver as if he produced the sounds of someone who was having a nervous breakdown. Maybe this was how karma would get him back for aiding and acting as an accomplice for Brenda Craiger. I know he lied, he knows he lied, and God knows he lied!

I should not wish anything negative on Dr. Marcel Nulldick because, as Bill Bellkoe explained it, he was forced to take the side of a principal working under him. Even if that principal was as evil as Brenda Craiger, he was forced to support her heinous actions over my truthful actions!

In reality, it was good that Dr. Marcel Nulldick fired me because it changed me in a good way. It made me realize how strong I could remain during times of professional adversity. Spiritually, it took me back to the truth. I practiced meditation as frequently as I could; it was the only way I could emotionally endure the hurt and pain that Brenda Craiger had bestowed upon me during the 2003–2004 academic year. If I had stayed at the Souless Area School District, I would have remained on a path that was leading nowhere. When I did not get hired during the fall of 2004, I completed my Master's degree. I was taking a big chance. The possibility of me ever getting hired again was very slight, but I took the chance, and the outcome was positive and pleasurable. My spiritual and inner wealth grew, and simultaneously my annual salary doubled when I was hired at another local public school district. Therefore, the fact that Dr. Marcel Nulldick fired me lead me to a spiritual and financial place that was so much better! I should write him a thank-you note! The words of the DJ on June 2, 2004 will be forever etched in my mind: "After today there will be sunny days ahead!" The entire scenario of emotional hurt and pain, induced by Brenda Craiger, lead to my professional dismissal. Mother Teresa teaches us that Jesus Christ is present in all sorts of disguises. It is just so difficult to think that Brenda Craiger could inflict such an enormous amount of emotional pain upon someone, and then the outcome for that person, me, was positive. In reality, that was exactly what happened! What Dr. Marcel Nulldick, Assistant Superintendent, gave me when he fired me was another opportunity to grow spiritually, emotionally, financially, and professionally.

Bertha Both was a Special Education Teacher with seventeen years of experience. She is number three on the list of heinous souls. She had been spread too thin from a special education workload, and she thought she could alleviate some of her workload and get away with it! I felt sorry for Bertha Both, because she was sneaky and underhanded. I felt sorry for her because she was an emotional person, but I still resented her for the backstabbing and sabotage actions against me. She just kept eating and eating! I would have been happy with a water bottle and a bathroom break. Bertha Both gave herself time every day in her schedule to assist me, however she never helped me. It was one big lie! She took advantage of me, over and over, for 180 days. The fact that I had to write all of her progress monitoring, attend some of the parent-teacher conferences, and teach eleven of the students on her caseload alleviated many of her job responsibilities.

I will resent the behaviors of Bertha, but I felt sorry for her because she never experienced how good it feels to help another person. If it had been the other way around, I would have enjoyed helping someone new to Special Education; I would have used everything that I had learned for seventeen years and experienced a great amount of joy when helping out! She never experienced the release of serotonin! She was professionally spread too thin—like all special education teachers—however this fact did not give her the right to take advantage of me. I remember Dr. Marcel

Nulldick's words regarding the victimization of Bertha Both: "And when that person did that to you, she put a noose around her neck." I wonder if he stuck to it, if he enforced those ideas—not letting Bertha Both take advantage of another teacher or an aide, and not allowing her to have a free afternoon at someone's expense! I know she lied, she knows she lied, and God knows she lied.

Shelly Mitchel, the Acting Supervisor of Special Education, saw the good in me. I know Shelly Mitchel liked my work; she was aware of the fact that I was dedicated to the profession, she had observed me in the classroom, checked my special education paperwork, and even attended a couple of my IEP meetings. I knew that she thought I was a good person and that when Dr. Marcel Nulldick fired me, she knew that he was doing so because he needed to support the wrongful actions of Brenda Craiger. I knew that Shelly Mitchel was aware that I was a hard worker and could have been an asset to the Souless Area School District's Special Education Department. I know her evaluations of me, based on her classroom and IEP meeting observations, were swayed by the directives of Dr. Marcel Nulldick! I know she could not document the positive qualities she saw in me because she wanted to keep her job. Shelly Mitchel and I had some characteristics in common; for example, we were both go-getters, dreamers, and very action oriented. In these respects, we shared similar personalities. I know Shelly Mitchel thought highly of me.

I had a conversation with her on April 5, 2004, regarding the different expectations in the two elementary buildings of the Souless Area School District. Shelly commented, "You can't keep everyone happy." Of course, "everyone" was defined as Brenda Craiger! I know she lied; she knows she lied; and God knows she lied.

One Last Cry for Honesty

I had been observed many times during the academic year—much more frequently than was required by state regulations, according to PDE. Dr. Marcel Nulldick was out of work due to the condition that older people sometimes develop known as detached retina. Eye surgery was required, and he therefore was absent from his place of employment for an extended time. I was told that during my observation/evaluation of April 15, 2004, performed by Brenda Craiger, that Dr. Marcel Nulldick would be present. I considered Dr. Marcel Nulldick to be the better person of the two—of course that is the same as saying he was better than Satan! Therefore I was happy to hear that the tyrant, Brenda Craiger, would have another professional in the classroom during my formal administrative observation/evaluation. Bill Bellkoe always looked over my materials and written lesson plans prior to any formal administrative observation/evaluation performed by Brenda Craiger or Dr. Marcel Nulldick. Therefore, I knew my lessons and instruction during my formal administrative observations/evaluations were solid! When I learned that Dr. Nulldick would be absent, I requested that Shelly Mitchel attend the observation period. I wrote the following note to Shelly Mitchel.

4/14/2004
Dear Shelly,
 Brenda is observing me on Thursday, 4/15/04, from 2:00 to 3:35 PM. If you would like to drop in, that would be great. I have given my lesson plans a great deal of thought. No matter what I do, or how well I deliver the instruction, Brenda will give me an unsatisfactory evaluation. I was told that Dr. Marcel Nulldick would

be accompanying Brenda for this evaluation. It is unfortunate for me that Marcel is out.

Brenda recently has not been as rude to me. I assume either you or Marcel told her to treat me differently.

The other day during our phone conversation, you stated that we were in the same boat—both overwhelmed. It was great to have you understand and empathize. However, our situations are not exactly the same. If I can't win over Brenda Craiger, I will not have a job. Even though I am aware of this, I continue to work hard and give all of my personal time to my job.

In September and in October I talked with Brenda Craiger and informed her that I felt my schedule was brutal. She immediately shrugged off my comments, and told me to talk to Dr. Lurk. Others told me to file a grievance because I had insufficient travel time and less than the contracted planning time. Someone told me to talk to Marcel Nulldick. A few days prior to Christmas break, I talked with Marcel Nulldick. Since that time, my Mountclair assignment has become even more difficult.

Thanks for calling me at home after my observation. Thanks for noticing that I am working hard. My morning at B. C. Patanjali Elementary School is intense, as the number of special education students have grown; my afternoon is equally intense.

Fondly,
Katrina

The fact that Shelly Mitchel, the Acting Supervisor of Special Education, thought highly of my professional work made me feel great, though it simultaneously made me even more frustrated with the entire scenario. I knew I was going to be dismissed, but I continued to work hard because I loved my students. They wrote me notes, hugged me, and sometimes brought little gifts like gum or candy and taped it to a friendly note. Whenever I questioned what was academically best for a student, I would ask myself one question: if this were my biological child, what would I want to have occurred in school?

Dishonesty Pinnacle

Dr. Marcel Nulldick, Assistant Superintendent, had no grounds for my dismissal because I fulfilled all professional responsibilities, even though I had been given an unfair workload and a schedule that violated my contract. It was necessary for Dr. Marcel Nulldick to prepare false documentation to use for grounds for my dismissal. Therefore, he asked Shelly Mitchel to join him in the false documentation. On April 27, 2004, Shelly Mitchel attended the IEP meeting scheduled by the school psychologist for the purpose of Tim Bella's dismissal from special education. This decision was based on several achievement test scores, some administered by the school psychologist in addition to the DAB (Diagnostic Achievement Battery-Third Edition), which I had administered on February 13, 2004. Several professionals attended this IEP meeting in addition to Mrs. Bella, Tim's mother. Due to the fact that the child was being dismissed from Special Education, the school psychologist included Shelly Mitchel, the Acting Supervisor of Special Education, as part of the team meeting. The dismissal NOREP (Notice of Recommended Educational Placement) form was documented and signed on April 27, 2004, by seven adults—all part of the IEP team for Tim Bella. When students are dismissed from Special Education, they no longer have an IEP. In preparation for Tim Bella's meeting, I frequently contacted Diane Ridgedan. She was aware of Tim Bella's progress and guided me on the preparation of his paperwork.

On May 18, 2004, during the final ITAP meeting, Dr. Marcel Nulldick mentioned his concern for Tim Bella's IEP. I verbally defended myself, explaining to him that the school psychologist had dismissed Tim Bella from Special Education. I also reminded the ITAP team that I had contacted Diane Ridgedan every step of the way when preparing for Tim

Bella's IEP meeting. Diane Ridgedan was part of the ITAP team and was seated next to me. I noticed the look of intensity on her face as I defended myself to the ITAP team. Diane was well aware of the fact this was simply one more act of dishonesty—but she needed her job and could not therefore defend me in front of the other professionals who were present. Diane Ridgedan looked frustrated—she knew exactly how Dr. Marcel Nulldick and Shelly Mitchel were conniving against me! Diane Ridgedan wanted justice! Following the ITAP meeting, Dr. Nulldick instructed Shelly Mitchel to prepare a documentation of lies.

On June 1, 2004, I received a memo from Shelly Mitchel that initially shocked me as I read it! Then I realized that Dr. Marcel Nulldick, Assistant Superintendent, had directed Shelly Mitchel to write such a document of false facts.

TO: Katrina Hall
FROM: Shelly Mitchel
RE: Review of IEPs for ITAP
DATE: 6/01/2004

On Monday, May 24, 2004, Diane Ridgedan and I reviewed a copy of Tim Bella's IEP. The following items need to be addressed on this copy of his IEP in order to be compliant with state and federal guidelines:

Part V—Present Levels:
There is no information that describes the student's achievement as related to specific skills and his response to curriculum to rationalize why he needs individual goals/objectives and specifically designed instruction.

Part V—Goals/Objectives:
If the student was experiencing reading difficulties, then a reading comprehension goal would be appropriate and a necessary component of the IEP and his reading instruction.

Part IX-—Specially Designed Instruction:
There is no SDI listed. All special education students need SDI to achieve their goals and objectives.

Part XV—Type of Service:
The correct type and percentage of special education services is important documentation that is mandatory for state reporting of delivery of services in the least restrictive environment.

Diane Ridgedan mentioned to me that there was a more recent version of Tim Bella's IEP based on some changes recommended by the school psychologist. I am currently waiting to receive this IEP and the most current IEP on your other students.

Thank you for your attention to this matter.

Dr. Marcel Nulldick used this as the one of the main reasons for my dismissal. He specifically mentioned the fact that I failed to prepare a well-written IEP for Tim Bella. Then he continued to mention that IEP writing is an integral part of the responsibilities of the Special Education teacher. Dr. Marcel Nulldick was forced to lie about my work because my work was solid. I know that all of my paperwork submitted to the district office was perfect. Prior to any meeting I always asked Diane Ridgedan to check over my paperwork because I was new to the profession. Diane always helped me, and therefore they could not find any mistakes in my special education documents. Dr. Marcel Nulldick submitted these lies to PDE (the Pennsylvania Department f Education).

Bill Bellkoe, Principal of B. C. Patanjali—I know that my life and Bill's life were supposed to be intertwined that year. It was Bill Bellkoe who brought me to this situation! I know that we were connected professionally for a divine reason. I know it took him some time to have faith in me professionally, but once he saw how hard I worked and how dedicated to the profession I remained, even during those weeks when I knew I was going to get fired, he thought highly of me both professionally and personally. On March 3, 2004, Wednesday, Bill and I were talking, and he stated, "That is what I like about you—whenever I tell you to do something, you always do it!" This statement shocked me because he was the principal, and therefore I was certainly going to do what he told me to do. Were there teachers in his building who did not do everything that he told them?

I even did everything that Brenda Craiger told me to do, and I hated her. After I did it, she frequently turned it around to hold against me in some heinous method—but I still did it! Sometimes I think Bill Bellkoe was overwhelmed by my honesty, but deep inside he saw that as a quality of mine! I had many conversations with Bill Bellkoe, and we shared our distaste for Brenda Craiger. When I announced that Brenda Craiger hated me, Bill said, "Well, she hates me too!" I felt sympathy for Brenda Craiger because she was isolated and unhappy. Diane Ridgedan had informed me that she thought Brenda Craiger was in some way excluded and isolated from the other administrators in the district. Furthermore, the reason for her isolation and exclusion was how she had mistreated me and many others. I was not the only teacher tortured by Brenda Craiger, and I feel that the other administrators disliked her because she was actively involved in numerous teacher vendettas. I also felt sympathy for her because she must be a very unhappy person--happy people do not become obsessed with the victimization of others!

It was my inner awareness that a principal as strong and experienced as Bill Bellkoe thought highly of me as a professional that gave me the strength to continue. I knew I had to go back to school every day for 180 days, and I continually reminded myself of this positive inner awareness. If I could professionally win over Bill Bellkoe, then I could be professionally successful in any other public school district. On more than one occasion Bill would help me prepare for one of my formal observations, specifically when I was preparing for Brenda Craiger's observations. And on one occasion, when I was preparing for Dr. Marcel Nulldick's formal observation, Bill helped me. Following the observations, I would return to Bill and show him the checked areas in which I needed improvement We would laugh because we both knew that I received unfair treatment. On one occasion, Bill told me he realized that I had four very different professionals to keep happy. He informed me that he realized that these four administrators wanted and expected very different things. He realized how difficult it was to keep everyone happy. I know how Bill treated me, he knows how he treated me, and God knows how he treated me!

Diane Ridgedan, a Special Education teacher and liaison, was a person of integrity! She knew that I was not going to win; no matter what I did, Brenda Craiger was going to have me fired. Diane stood by me during all the tough times. She wanted to tell me more, but she would say "Katrina ... My job" She knew that I had been taken advantage of and that I had so much to learn about Special Education, and she always helped me both professionally and emotionally. Positive things will happen to her! Diane Ridgedan and I shared a more developed spiritual level of existence than anyone else that I had associated with in the Souless Area School District. Diane Ridgedan had more emotional intelligence and positive energy than anyone else. It was great to be in the same room with Diane because we understood each other. She knew I had been handed an unfair workload; she knew I had been screwed over and given a bum deal. She saw through Brenda Craiger and was well aware of the sabotage and undermining that had occurred. She also knew that Brenda Craiger would be punished for her unethical behaviors—each time Brenda Craiger victimized me, Brenda would attract negativity of some sort into her own life! Diane and I discussed things like this. Diane had witnessed people being dismissed from the Souless Area School District "in such a disgrace!" She also witnessed me being dismissed after having worked so hard. I wish Dr. Marcel Nulldick had not directed Diane to have no contact with me because I wanted us to remain lifelong friends! I know Diane defended me to the big wigs; I know she told the administrators of the Souless Area School District that they were dismissing a good employee. I know how she treated me, she knows how she treated me, and God know how she treated me! Diane Ridgedan was an angel in my life during the 2003–2004 academic year!

"Angles and ministers of grace defend us."
—William Shakespeare, *Hamlet*, act I, scene iv.

Pleasurable Moments

Even though my experience was filled with emotional adversity, I had many pleasurable moments. I loved teaching and I loved the children. I loved the notes that they wrote to me, and I have saved those notes. I loved the post it notes that Bill Bellkoe would leave on my desk after a walkthrough observation, and I have saved those notes. The most fulfilling and positive experience that I had was observing a student understand something for the first time. I watched Gary significantly increase his vocabulary and his reading fluency. I taught Tim to do long division, and we shared a feeling of elation the day he got it. Even though his regular education teacher took credit for it at his dismissal IEP meeting, I know that I was the teacher who patiently worked with him until he got it! One day Gary and I shared a feeling of excitement because I allowed him to complete his own fluency chart, and he was able to help me keep track of his progress in reading. Sometimes we celebrated with treats, or the children would eat their lunch in my room rather than going outside to recess. They loved being in my room, and I loved having them in my room. Sometimes if one of my B. C. Patanjali students were having a bad day, they would come to my classroom to vent to me, and I would always give them a hug! If someone had bullied them, or if their best friend sat with someone else at lunch, they told me. They shared with me their feelings of sadness because they knew I would listen and then try to comfort them. My students trusted me, and I loved them. I loved teaching and I loved the children!

The Perfect School:
B. C. Patanjali Elementary School

B. C. Patanjali was the most perfect elementary school in the state of Pennsylvania. Early in the academic year, I had an IEP meeting in which Dr. Lurk and Bill Bellkoe were present. After the meeting, I informed the student's father that she was in good hands because her child attended B. C. Patanjali Elementary School. I referred to B. C. Patanjali as "The perfect school, in a perfect world, with a perfect principal!" Dr. Lurk laughed and asked me, "How much did Bill Bellkoe pay you to say that?" Later in the academic year, during one of my numerous meetings with Dr. Marcel Nulldick, I referred to B. C. Patanjali as the perfect school. I asked Dr. Marcel Nulldick, "B. C. Patanjali is the perfect school, isn't it?" He replied, "Yes, it is." When I think about the numerous conversations we had, especially toward the end of the year, they were friendly. Dr. Nulldick was not phony like Brenda Craiger—we actually, in some strange way, had a rapport. He even told me that if he had been there in September, 2003, things would have been different for me. I wonder if he would make a statement like that during litigation! It was an honest statement on his part, and I respected him for making such an honest statement. I imagine that I might still be working in the Souless Area School District if I had never been assigned to Brenda Craiger's building.

Dr. Marcel Nulldick and I would frequently meet at B. C. Patanjali and discuss a Brenda Craiger initiated complaint about me. One of the B. C. Patanjali teachers approached me one day near the end of the academic year, due to the frequent appearances of the assistant superintendent in the building of B. C. Patanjali Elementary School. She asked, "Katrina, is everything okay with your job? I get a little worried when I see Marcel in this building so much."

I explained to her, "No, everything is not okay, and I am going to be fired very soon." She was shocked with my statement and shocked with my honesty. Then I explained some of the details—how Brenda Craiger and Bertha Both had treated me.

The Notes

As the end of the year approached, I experienced a great deal of sadness because I had developed a positive student-teacher relationship with the twenty students with which I had worked. The students liked me, and a lot of teaching and learning had taken place.

The notes from the children were very pleasurable to read. My favorite one was from Mindy Rissmiller.

October 10-30-03
Dear Mrs. Hall

I love working for you and you are a good pirson. I would like it if i could stay in your room more often but i have other things to do. I like what you are teaching me this year. I like fithe grade. I am not good at spelling and other things. But i like staing with you because you give me candy and sota and a lot of things. if you ever have to leav you can tell me wheir you are going and I can right to you and you can right to me. I realy liked when you give things to everybody even if thay be bad. i thought that was real nice. I will see you on Monday!!

Siselery,
Mindy

Mindy drew decorations on the letter including a hand, a heart, and a starfish, and she traced her own hand and drew rings on two of her fingers. I loved this letter! Mindy made her own envelope and wrote, " to Miss , Hall from Mindy Rissmiller." She decorated the envelope with a picture of a spaceship and taped a packet of Sweetarts on it. Mindy Rissmiller will always have a special place in my heart because she had a very difficult home life. At one point she and mother were homeless and lived in a car. They also moved to different low-rent trailers from time to time. It was very sad. Mindy was fairly intelligent. When I administered the DAB to Mindy, I shared her scores with Diane Ridgedan. Diane replied, "Well, we will just refer to Mindy as a 'victim of circumstance' special education student." Certainly if Mindy had come from a better home, she would have made adequate academic progress. When I think about Mindy, I think that *I made a difference to that one!*

One of the Mountclair students wrote the following note:

<u>Mrs. Hall</u>
you are a good reading teacher and thank you for giving us lots of stikers and lots food
From: Sally Vard

On Valentine's Day one of the Mountclair students gave me a card telling me how awesome I was.

On the last day of school for students, one of the B. C. Patanjali parents brought her daughter to school. Mrs. Chem accompanied her daughter to my classroom and gave me flowers and a beautiful card that they had created together on the computer. It was color printed, and the inside panel recited a verse from the Bible: " …With thanksgiving let your requests be made known unto God. Philippians 4:6." Beneath this biblical verse was a colorful picture of a stained glass window. The main panel contained the following note: "*Thoughtfulness like yours is appreciated more than words can say. I will miss you over the summer. I am looking forward to seeing you next year. Love, Shannon Chem.*"

This was heartbreaking because I could not tell Shannon or her mother what had happened and that I would no longer be Shannon's special education teacher next year. I had enjoyed working with Shannon because she was delightful and appreciative of my support. I knew she was fond of me and enjoyed working with me in my classroom because I made her feel comfortable in her learning environment. As her mother handed me this note, she verbalized how much little Shannon had learned from me, and she thanked me over and over. Teary eyed, I showed this note to Diane Ridgedan; she just shook her head in regret of my situation.

Purpose for Writing This Book: Resolution

I sincerely hope that this book is read by people who have the power both emotionally and financially to produce a change. This is a true story; these things actually happened to me in a public school in the state of Pennsylvania. The actions of the main characters are heinous; simultaneously their entire demeanor lacks emotional intelligence. I watched administrators lie—just out and out lie— both verbally and on documents that they submitted to the Pennsylvania Department of Education. The PSEA Voice article written by John Audi, which I have quoted, mentions laws that could be the basis of change. I am well aware that I am not the only teacher to whom this has happened. I am also well aware of the fact that the best teacher in the world could receive a negative evaluation, skewed by the sole fact that an administrator dislikes that specific teacher.

Everything in quotation marks is true—these statements were actually made to me sometime during my 180 days of professional adversity. All the letters are actual documents, with only name changes for legal purposes. Mother Teresa has taught us that the smallest thing done with love can change the world. I have written this book from a spiritual place of love. I do not want my professional suffering to have been in vain. I have tried to look back on the experience with strength and forgiveness to those who were so intentionally hurtful and vindictive. If any of my tones seem somewhat blatant or harsh I apologize to the reader. It was challenging to remain positive toward the characters under the circumstances which created 180 DAYS. This book has been written based on a true life experience which was devastating to me. I was innocent and constantly needed to defend my innocence through documentation of details submitted to administrators.

After this experience I have worked on moving to a place of forgiveness and harmony. It has been extremely difficult to forgive those who victimized me. It is my goal that this book will help future teachers avoid professional adversity, and this goal helps me to look upon this experience with love and forgiveness. Part of me would like to confront the professionals who victimized me. I have visualized myself in a room with these professionals, making direct eye contact with them, and asking them in a calm and harmonious tone why they behaved in an unethical manner. From a redemptive aspect I know that I must let go of this desire. I realized that I had been taken advantage of professionally and domestically. I also realized that I needed to change my thinking and therefore change the adversity in my professional and personal life. Dr. Wayne Dyer has taught us that changing one's thinking automatically changes the things that happen in one's daily life. Furthermore, this book has been a process of catharsis in my life.

Working for 180 days under the conditions stated in this book can be compared to being emotionally struck by lightning! The personal result was that I became a stronger and more mature person. The professional result was that I was hired in a public school district where my salary was doubled and a strong union was in existence.

I have a vision for a resolution. Legal issues need to be addressed. There is a need for public school administrators to abide by more strict laws. First, the misconduct codes must be implemented for all professionals, inclusively for both teachers and administrators. I have spoken to several attorneys who have informed me that this situation of sabotage occurs frequently. I have learned that teachers can be dismissed based on petty items or out and out lies, if they happen to get on the bad side of an administrator. Second, the misconduct codes need to be updated and in some areas rewritten. Third, when a misconduct code is submitted to the state department of education, immediate investigation needs to be completed. If necessary, reprimands or dismissals should follow the immediate investigation. Finally and most significantly, there is a need to implement a law that requires all formal observations and evaluations of teachers performed by public school administrators to be video recorded. This video recording should be submitted to the state department of education, because it is mandated.

Such a law should have been implemented years ago due to the fact that teacher observations are subjective. Even in ideal situations, the perception of the observer is subjective! Such a law would help teachers in extreme situations who have been subjected to heinous actions of administrative personnel.

Resolution: Please Listen

I have spoken to numerous attorneys, and numerous teachers, in preparation for writing this book. Unfortunately, it is common knowledge that when administrators do not have a positive professional rapport with a teacher, they automatically skew the evaluation of that teacher. When the formal observation is actively taking place, there are no witnesses, there are no videos, and only students are present in the classroom. There is a need for legal change in the public school system of procedures for formal administrative observations/evaluations, specifically for nontenured teachers.

All formal observations should be video recorded because administrators are able to skew observations/evaluations. Typically there are no witnesses (except the students) and the administrative observations are subjective. The Pennsylvania Department of Education should mandate the submission of video recordings of formal administrative observations. A Union Representative should be present during any formal administrative classroom observation, and union representation should be mandated.

If any part of this account seems redundant I apologize to the reader. The redundancy is due to the intensity of my quest to be heard. If people of integrity really listen to this message the necessary changes will occur.

A Test of Human, Emotional Strength:
Good-bye to Me

One day at B. C. Patanjali Elementary School, after I had gotten fired, the music teacher stopped into by my classroom #112 to say good-bye to me. Everyone knew that I had gotten fired, because word travelled fast in such a small district. When the music teacher stopped to bid me farewell on June 8, 2004, we had a short but memorable conversation. She wished me good luck. I thanked her for stopping in and lamented that I had worked so hard but still had been fired. I also lamented that there were many times when I thought that emotionally I could not make it until the end, June 8, 2004, because Brenda Craiger had professionally tortured me! The music teacher replied, "Well, that just shows how strong you are!" This statement has stuck in my mind because I have remained strong in the face of adversity during times of professional, emotional, domestic, marital, and financial adversity. I hope this book can stimulate some change and that my 180 days of professional adversity and suffering and emotional adversity and suffering have not been in vain.

Writing this book will help to provide me with some closure, catharsis, and redemption from my 180 days of suffering from the victimization of Brenda Craiger, Dr. Marcel Nulldick, and Bertha Both. I have forgiven Shelly Mitchell, Supervisor of Special Education, because I know she was swayed by Dr. Marcel Nulldick. I also know she thought highly of me; my instruction was fine, my special education paperwork was well done, and she knew I was a dedicated teacher and a hard worker. Also, I knew that Shelly Mitchell and Bill Bellkoe had spoken about my unfortunate situation at Mountclair Elementary School when I was not present.

I have grown from this experience and am therefore a better person. My spiritual wealth and inner wealth have doubled. The outcome is pleasurable because I have been lead to something better. Because I have grown, when I touch others who need help, I will have more to offer. This trauma in my life caused an internal change in me, and with this change came richness. I was changed in a good way, and it has taken me back to the truth. I am able to help many students and their parents because I have lived through such emotional and professional trauma. It has led me to something so much better both internally and externally.

Finally, I feel that each individual has a mission to fulfill during his or her physical lifespan on this planet. I feel that my 180 days of professional adversity and writing this book as a plea for legal change are part of my life's work.

As Sylvia Browne says, "…what doesn't kill us makes us stronger."

Contact The Author

Anyone wishing to contact the author may do so at the following e-mail address: **days180kh@yahoo.com** .

Anyone wishing to write to the author may do so at the following postal address:

Crystal E. Emerson
Post Office Box 126524
Harrisburg, Pennsylvania 17112

Author Credits

Thank you Mom.

Thank you Gwen.

Thank you Josh.

Thank you Aden.

Thank you Mackenzie.

Thank you A.J.

Thank you Emerson.

Thank you Allan.

Thank you Tommy.

Thank you Emerald.

Thank you WC, DD

Thank you BM, MH-P

Thank you KK.

Thank you, thank you.

I love you!

About the Author

Crystal E. Emerson has worked in the public school system in the state of Pennsylvania for several years. Crystal holds a Bachelor of Science Degree in Secondary Education, a Master's of Education with a specialty in Special Education, a teaching certificate in English, and a teaching certificate in Special Education.

Crystal has experienced the unethical behavior of administrators and other professionals while working in a public school district in the state of Pennsylvania. It is Crystal's hope that her 180-day experience of emotional adversity, sabotage, and undermining has not occurred in vain.

Crystal's down-to-earth account of her employment during the 2003–2004 academic year in a public school in the state of Pennsylvania is a work of truth, honesty, integrity, and emotional and professional adversity.

Crystal resides in Pennsylvania with her family. Crystal continues to work in a public school district as a Special Education Teacher.